Hein Severloh in 1944, as a 20 year-old soldier, and in 2002 at age 79.

Heinrich (Hein) Severloh, was born June 23, 1923 in Metzingen, in the Celle district of the Lüneburger Heide (Lueneburger Heath). His parents were the farmer, mayor and Ortsbauernführer (head of the official local farmers' organization), Heinrich Severloh, and Frieda Gries Severloh. He was the second of three children and the eldest son (with a three-year older sister and a six-year younger brother) and the eleventh of his line named Heinrich. He was from the old Lower Saxon family, Severloh (named for the village, Severloh, in the south heath) whose roots reach back to the time of the Thirty Years' War.

From 1928 to 1937 Heinrich Severloh attended the local school, then, until 1940, the vocational training school, and in the winters of 1940/41 and 1941/42, the agricultural school in Celle. From age 11 to 14 he was a member of the German Youth. In July, 1942, at the age of 19, he was drafted for the military, went first to Russia then, at the end of 1943, to France, and survived the first day of the invasion of Normandy.

In 1949 he married Elisabeth Schliephake, from Rautheim near Brunswick. This marriage produced two sons and two daughters. In 1953 he took over the family farm, which he passed on to his eldest son in 1971, and thereafter until 1989 was an independent insurance agent.

Translator's Note

Heinrich Severloh was stationed at Widerstandsnest (WN) 62, one of 15 such on *Omaha Beach*. Widerstandsnest is translated literally as "resistance nest", an awkward and unfamiliar term in English, which knows of snipers' nests and machine gun nests, but not of resistance nests. I have translated this as "strongpoint". The Germans, who tend to be more specific about these things, differentiate a Widerstandsnest (resistance nest) and a Stützpunkt (strongpoint) - a strongpoint has a completement of at least a full company. However, the fortified position known as WN 62 was not only heavily entrenched, but contained several artillery pieces in hardened, reinforced concrete bunkers, as well as an artillery observation post and underground troop quarters - also constructed of reinforced concrete. It would seem, in western terms, to be a strongpoint.

While equivalent U.S. and German grades of commissioned officers coincide neatly, that is not always the case with enlisted grades. The German "Gefreiter" is often translated as "Lance Corporal", but no such grade existed in the U.S. Army during World War II. The rank is generally assigned almost automatically after a certain period of time and does not seem to have any command responsibilities associated with it. It seems, therefore, to be the functional equivalent of a U.S. Private First Class (Pfc.) of that time, and I have translated it accordingly. British readers might be more comfortable with "Lance Corporal".

I have used the following equivalent (artillery) ranks from U.S. War Department publications:

Wachtmeister	Technical Sergeant (T/Sgt.)
	Master Sergeant (M/Sgt.) or
	First Sergeant (1st Sgt.) depending on function
Feldwebel	Staff Sergeant (S.Sgt.)
Unterfeldwebel	Sergeant (Sgt.)
Unteroffizier	Corporal (Cpl.)

The area immediately above the tidal beach is given in German as "Vorstrand", which translates literally into English as "foreshore", but is a term unfamiliar to most American readers. I have translated the German "Vorstrand" as "upper beach". The gradient between the tidal beach and the upper beach in most WWII literature is given as "shingle bank", and this is a term familiar to British, but not American readers. The term has been adopted by most writers, perhaps because the planning for *Operation Overlord* (the Normandy invasion) was done in England and it was the term used in the planning documents. "Shingle", as used in this connection, refers to a beach composed of pebbles or gravel, rather than simply sand. In this stretch of *Omaha Beach*, the bank between the tidal beach and the upper beach consisted, as described by Severloh, of palm-sized stones, or gravel. I have translated "Kieselbank" or "Kiesbett" (shingle bank) as "gravel bank".

The incident of the LCI(L) landing on *Omaha Beach* at 0630, in advance of the first wave of landing craft, has been questioned by some writers; it is not reported in official U.S. accounts of *D-Day*, and there is speculation that such an incident may have occurred at a different time.

Robert R. Wolf

Fifth English edition, 2017.

First German edition published in 2000
First English edition published in 2011
Second English edition 2013
Third English edition 2015
Fourth English edition 2016
by H.E.K.Creativ Verlag, Garbsen, Germany.

WN 62
A German Soldier's Memories of the Defense of Omaha Beach
Normandy, June 6, 1944
Hein Severloh
in cooperation with Helmut Konrad von Keusgen

Translation by Robert R. Wolf 2007

Copyrights by H.E.K.Creativ Verlag

Hein Severloh: Additional information regarding
www.hek-creativ-verlag.de and **www.von-keusgen.de**

Maps, layout, graphic construction and cover:
Helmut Konrad Freiherr von Keusgen
Print: Jelgavas Tipografija
Printed in Latvija 2017

ISBN 978-3-932922-23-7

WN 62

Hein Severloh

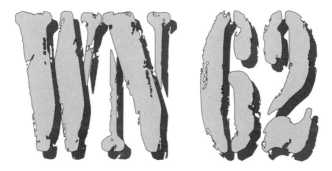

A German Soldier's Memories
of the Defense of Omaha Beach
Normandy, June 6, 1944

Hein Severloh
Translation by Robert R. Wolf

First Lieutenant Bernhard Frerking - Normandy 1944

Comrades grave
Bernhard Frerking / Karl Kleinpaß
La Cambe / Normandy

Dedicated to
1st Lt. Bernhard Frerking,
my comrades killed in action
and the Americans who died in front of WN 62

With the author of military history and D-Day expert, Helmut Konrad Freiherr von Keusgen, at the U.S. Military Cemetery in Colleville, only 500 meters from the former WN 62, and in connection with one of four trips to Normandy during our work on this book. Nobody can really imagine, how terrible one feel, when a quarter of these 9,386 crosses stress one's own conscience.

Contents

The Normandy with the five landing sectors of the Allies

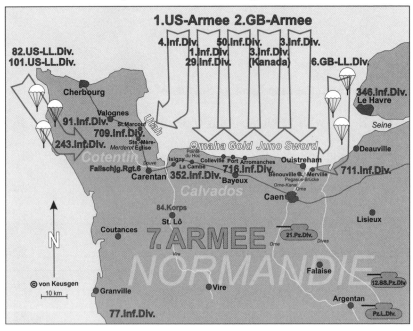

15 German Strongpoints *(Widerstandsnest=WN)* at Omaha Beach

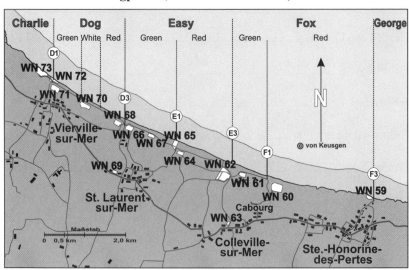

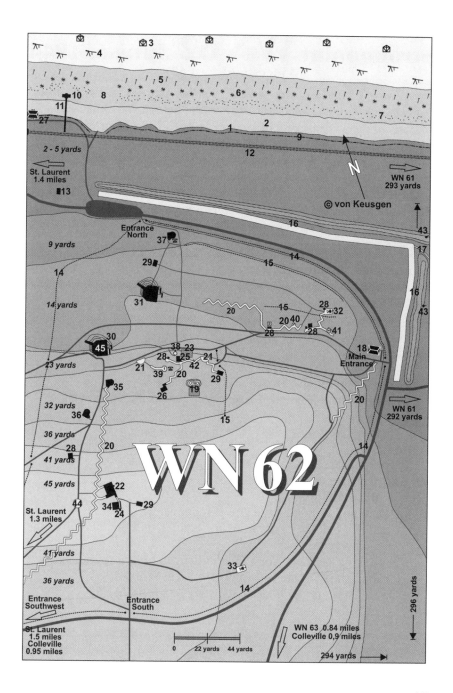

2 - 5 yards

St. Laurent
1.4 miles

WN 61
293 yards

© von Keusgen

N

9 yards

Entrance
North

14

14 yards

23 yards

32 yards

36 yards

41 yards

45 yards

St. Laurent
1.3 miles

41 yards

36 yards

Entrance
Southwest

Entrance
South

St. Laurent
1.5 miles
Colleville
0.95 miles

WN 61
292 yards

WN 62

WN 63 0.84 miles
Colleville 0,9 miles

294 yards

296 yards

0   22 yards   44 yards

Main
Entrance

Strongpoint **WN 62** June 6, 1944
(**W**iderstand**s**nest 62)

…one of 15 strongpoints on the 3.75 miles-long bay, site of the American Omaha sectors, Dog, Easy and Fox was permanently manned by 28 soldiers of the 3rd Company of Grenadier Regiment 726 of the 716th Infantry Division. Soldiers of this company were divided between Strongpoint WN 59 to WN 64; the company command post was located in WN 63, 1,225 yards to the rear. On June 6, 1944, there were, in addition, 13 soldiers of the 1st Battery, 1st Battalion of Artillery Regiment 352 of the 352nd Infantry Division *(positioned in Houtteville, 2.8 miles inland)* stationed at the artillery observation post in WN 62.

Key to Map *(see page 17)*

Topographic Measurements

1 = Average 1.5 meters high, steep embankment separating the upper and the tidal beaches.

2 = 6 to 8 meters wide bank of largely hand-sized gravel (often translated as "shale" or shingle")

Beach Obstacles

3 = Element C *("Belgian Gates")*

4 = Ramp racks, some with saw teeth and mines

5 = Wooden posts *("Rommel's Asparagus")* often furnished with a mine at the tip.

6 = Cruciform steel obstacles *("Czech Hedgehogs")*

7 = Mines

8 = Minefield passages, to be able to reach the beach

9 = Mined border with trip wire fuses

Technical Installations

10 = Gravel mill to grind large gravel for concrete.

11 = Conveyor belt for transport of crushed gravel from the mill to the field railway (see 12)

12 = Narrow gauge tracks for a field railway to transport sand and crushed gravel to the construction sites at WN 61.

13 = Deutz Diesel motor to drive the conveyor (on a V-belt).

14 = Outer barbed wire area.

15 = Inner barbed wire area.

16 = Water filled anti-tank ditch, 1.7 meters deep and 4 meters wide, with built-up earthen bank.

17 = Channel to supply water to the anti-tank ditch.
18 = Former beach villa; used as guardroom, quarters and kitchen for 3rd Company, 726th Infantry Regiment.
19 = Excavation and excavated material for a planned new guardroom.
20 = Circa 1.7 meters deep protected area communication trenches.
21 = Concrete platforms on which the two Czech 7.65 cm field pieces were located before they were installed in the new casemates *(see 30 and 31)*.
22 = Underground troop quarters bunker for 20 soldiers.
23 = Location of former half-buried troop quarters and a wooden barracks that served as quarters until the completion of the new troop bunker *(see 22)*.
24 = Bunker for a radio as well as a Light Beam Transceiver, for communication with Strongpoints WN 61 and WN 63.
25 = Observation post and fire direction position for the forward observer of Artillery Regiment 352 and for the 1st Battery, stationed 4.5 kilometers inland at Houtteville *(Fire control officer: 1st Lt. Bernhard Frerking, killed in action June 6th; deputy fire control officer: Second Lt. Grass, missing in action from June 6th; radio operator: T/.Sgt. Ewald Fack, killed in action June 6th, at Mandeville)*.
26 = Radio bunker for the fire control position *(see 25)* of Artillery Regiment 352.*(Corporal Beermann, missing in action since June 6th; Private Kurt Wernecke, wounded near WN 62, June 6th; Private Herbert Schulz, wounded at WN 62 on June 6th, died June7th; as well as two radiomen, whose names are not known)*.
27 = Former beach villa used as an observation post for surveillance of the sea by 6 naval infantry soldiers, with a radio.
28 = Ammunition bunker
29 = Latrines
Defensive Positions and Weapons
30 = Upper casemate for a Czech 7.65 cm field piece Model 1917.
31 = Lower casemate for a Czech 7.65 cm field piece *(as above)*.
32 = Open field position for a 5 cm anti-tank gun.
33 = Open field position for a 5 cm anti-tank gun *(with four gunners of an anti-tank company of Grenadier Regiment 916 of the 352nd Infantry Division, whose fate is unknown)*.
34 = Double Tobruk position for a machine gun on a swivel mount, and a 5 cm mortar *(neither weapon was installed as of June 6th)*.
35 = Tobruk position for 5 cm mortar.
36 = Tobruk position for 5 cm mortar.
37 = Tobruk position for machine gun, Model 1934, on a swivel mount *(with a telephone)*.

38 = Open, unhardened dugout position for a machine gun, Model 1934.

39 = Open, unhardened dugout position for a double machine gun, Model 1934, for anti-aircraft defense *(with telephone)*.

40 = Open, unhardened dugout position for a water-cooled Polish machine gun, Model 1917, on a swivel mount.

41 = Covered dugout bunker for a water-cooled Polish machine gun, Model 1917, on a swivel mount, as well as a control for two defensive flame throwers.

42 = Open field position for a machine gun, Model 1942 *(Private Heinrich Severloh)*.

43 = Defensive flame thrower.

Monuments

44 = Location of 1st U.S. Infantry Division monument.

45 = Location of 5th U.S. Engineer Special Brigade monument.

Forward

The 6th of June, 1944, the day of the large invasion of Normandy by the Allies, has influenced my entire later life. The young son of a farmer, I was drafted, and after early, horrible experiences in Russia, sent to Normandy. The invasion began 17 days before my 21st birthday. At that time there were many circumstances and contexts of which I was ignorant or had only an inadequate understanding. Much of the knowledge and understanding about which I can report today, I acquired only much later.

My autobiography is in no way an apology or justification; I am much more interested in describing honestly the events that have influenced me and my life. At that time, just as many others, I became a soldier against my will, and it became inevitable under these circumstances that I had, strenuously, to defend my life. I had no feeling of personal hatred for the enemy, but I fought instinctively with all my strength to survive when I was attacked, even as any other living creature. When, after the war, the first article about the Normandy invasion appeared in a magazine, my name was mentioned. After that something began to escalate, as a result of which I achieved a certain notoriety, the reason for which, sadly, I cannot imagine.

Since the first publication of this book in October, 2000, three complete printings have already been sold. But since then, a number of things have occurred related to June 6, 1944 and my life. I have, for this reason, included additional text and photographic material in the fourth printing, which brings my story up to date - but it will be the last, since at the age of 81 I have retired fully.

With this book I was able, as I realized with a great deal of joy, to have an effect - particularly on the hearts of many readers, even those of my former "enemies"... The reaction to my reminiscences has been overwhelming. I had not at first expected any such, and one cannot expect more. I thank all my readers and wish for them and for posterity, finally, lasting peace and understanding among the peoples of the earth.

Heinrich Severloh, February, 2005

21

The Long Road to WN 62

"It's starting!"

My Battery Commander, First Lieutenant Bernhard Frerking, had come into my small attic room at the rural estate of the Legrand family at Houtteville and awakened me.

"Come on, Hein; I have had a telephone message that it's starting! Imminent Danger...!"

This was the highest alert level. I jumped out of bed and dressed as quickly as I could. When I looked at my wristwatch it read midnight exactly. At that moment began the 6th of June of the year 1944...

The sky, darkened for the past several days by thick clouds, had cleared, and the sallow light of the full moon illuminated the rough, uneven landscape of Normandy. The cool night air was filled with the dull, alarming drone of the Allied bombers flying in from the sea further west. I was inwardly completely calm, and at the "Protze" *(as we called the squad responsible for the horses and limbers of our battery)* called to the nearby farmstead that they should send over a horse cart as quickly as possible for the commander of our 1st Battery, whose "orderly" I was. We had to hurry to the coast, four-and-a-half kilometers away, and to the artillery observation post at Strongpoint WN 62. Since I had been assigned as a machine gunner, and my machine gun was ready near the observation post, I had to accompany First Lieutenant Frerking there as his security. I was happy to be with him, as we had a good relationship. It was only a few minutes until the charrette arrived *(one of the large two-wheeled carriages with a folding top typical of the area, pulled by only one horse, or a donkey)*.

The two of us drove alone through Surrain, around St. Laurent to the east, to drive down the (over fifty meters high) sloping coastal bluff to get directly to Strongpoint WN 62. We were aware that the invasion would come; it had been expected for a long time, and there was much that had pointed to it in recent days. Only one week before something noteworthy had happened:

At the estate where we were quartered 1st Lt. Frerking had a bedroom, and a sitting room that he often called a casino. In this sitting room there was always a box, for which only the 1st Lieutenant had a key. On Tuesday, May 30th, I was ordered by my commander to go to his sitting room and guard important papers that lay open on the table. He had said, as he suddenly and quickly had to leave:

"Hein, look after the papers that are on the table. I don't have any time to lock them in the box."

I found these papers lying on the table in Frerking's work room; on the first page there was a conspicuous stamp: *Top Secret!* Written on the paper:

"Ship concentration in southern English harbors!"

Only two days later, on Thursday, June 1st, there was again, and quite openly, a new message on the table - again stamped *Top Secret.* This time the text read:

"The ships in the English harbors are being loaded!"

It was clear to me that Frerking intended to warn me in this way...

The next day, all the soldiers of our unit were ordered back to the limber park area in Mandeville, even the cannoneers *(except for the weapon guards).* Then, in Mandeville, our unit commander, Major Werner Pluskat, addressed the troops. He spoke of the need to fulfill our duty, and used the usual motivational expressions, but his words left the impression of an impending attack. Usually such speeches always ended with the formula "...until the last drop of blood..." *(by which it was to be made clear to the soldiers that there should be no surrender),* but Pluskat found new, never-before-heard words for the close of his speech:

"...A stinking corpse won't serve the fatherland..."

Major Werner Pluskat, the commander of the 1st Detachment of Artillery Regiment 352 of the 352nd Infantry Division.

I had pricked up my ears... Then, on the same day, 1st Lt. Frerking told the cook to prepare a special meal for the battery on the coming Sunday, and ordered him to get a side of beef. On Sunday we would be able to eat as much as we wanted, and red cabbage and potatoes were added to the unusually large portions of meat. It was all consumed. Since I already had an inkling of what was to come, this feast seemed to me like a last supper. This premonition had been with me ever since furloughs had been suspended at the end of April, on the 27th of the month, and I had shared it with my sister in a short letter I had written her for her birthday...

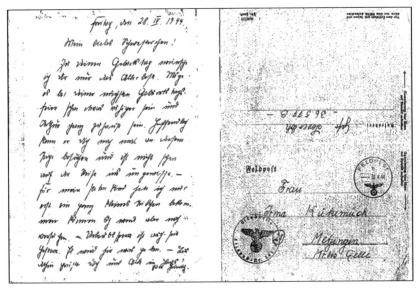

It was not at all unknown to the German side, that the landing offensive of the Allies was imminent, as one could see from a letter of April 28, 1944, to my sister (five weeks before the invasion):
My dear little sister! I wish you all the best for your birthday. For your next birthday celebration may it already be somewhat quieter, with Arthur at home. I hope he will still be able to be with you on this day and isn't already on his way to God knows where. For my godchild I have only just been able to get a little something. But I will try some more. Leaves are a also suspended as of yesterday. Something is going to happen here. Until then, my best to you and all at home   *Your Heinrich*

Now I headed our little carriage through the night down the road that had become familiar to us, and one could hear, from all around, the increasing drone of the enemy bombers. An eerie, ominous mood, but I was still not yet nervous or upset; I thought much more about how it had happened that on this cool night, and at this moment I was sitting on a small French carriage and was driving my officer across the steep coast to our observation post at WN 62...

I had been drafted on July 23, 1942, at the age of nineteen. Since I was unable to enlist in the navy or air force, I had decided on service in the army, and was assigned to Light Artillery Replacement Training Battalion 19 at the Scharnhorst Barracks at Hanover-Bothfeld. My ID bore the number 2295. At Hanover I first had to complete a short course of basic and mounted training.

My first photograph as a 19 year-old Artillery Private, and my ID.

In our unit we also had a bunch of Poles and Upper Silesians, who were known as "Volksdeutsche", or "ethnic Germans" who, nevertheless, didn't speak a word of German. But they were regular fellows and good comrades. That they should show some enthusiasm for the German fatherland was an absurdity.

One day, as we were marching, the order came to sing:

"A song!"

Since I was the tallest, and was at the front, the so-called flank man (Guidon bearer in the U.S. Army), I called out the song:

"The Blue Dragoons!"

Then we three Germans started singing, but the fifteen others were silent: they weren't even able to say "Good Day" in German. Then came the order from our sergeant:

"Hit the ground!"

The three of us in front did as he said. The Poles, however, now tried to march right over us. At first they didn't understand why we were lying

25

there so suddenly. Then they understood and also threw themselves down. Just at that time, however, the sergeant called out:

"Get up! A Song!"

So the three of us got up again, resumed our march, and began to sing *The Blue Dragoons,* but the other fifteen stayed where they were on the ground...

During our mounted training the order was given:

"Mount up!"

Then we three, who understood the order, got up on the horses. Only when we were mounted had the Poles finally actually understood what had been meant, and now also began to climb up on their horses. When the first one was half way up, an order came again:

"Dismount!"

So we got down while the others were still trying to get up. No one had taught these people the most important German terms. Despite the frequent comical situations, I found it really tragic. I was really sorry for the Poles.

On August 2, 1942, in a replacement transfer battalion, I was sent by train to Goslar on the Harz *(mountain)*, and was quartered with about 200 troops in a meeting room of the Hotel Hubertushof. After additional battalions had been assembled in Goslar during the following days, we traveled by train to northern France and arrived at St. Aubin, near Calais, on the 9th of August. I was assigned to the 3rd Battery of Artillery Regiment 321 of the 321st Infantry Division. Our real training only actually began there, but only two days later I reported to the division infirmary located at Champagne, with rheumatic pain that I had acquired on the trip. But I was sent back to my battery only ten days later. I had an abbreviated training as a mounted messenger.

On November 27th we moved out on the way to the entrainment terminal at Abbeville, and occupied quarters in Le Titre on the way. We were loaded up on December 2nd and our train went in the direction of Russia. On December 12th we were disembarked at Kovno, in Poland, to exercise the horses that for the ten days of the trip had stood crowded in the train cars. The ground was covered with snow and it was ice cold. We had a taste of the dreaded Russian winter...

Two days later, we started out again, and after another week we were unloaded in Bedlitza, in Russia. The next day we began our march to our destination, which lay in the middle section of the eastern front. A grey

A break at Kovno. Men and horses had to move around again after ten long days of travel.

sky had dulled the sun, and we toiled over an almost endless, flat desert of snow. The snow was a meter high, and drifts reached heights of four to five meters. A relentless, light snow fell, and our breath froze on our faces. By dint of great exertion we had put about fifty kilometers behind us by evening. The next day was just as awful. It was Christmas Eve, and we slogged through a remorseless winter with the temperature minus 30° centigrade (-22° F). When we stopped again to clear the road of a drift, one of our 150 troops had cut down a fir, and we put some "Hindenburg Lights" *(tallow candles)* in the snow. Then we gathered around and sang Christmas carols. We felt like crying.

Finally, on the 26th, we reached our position near Slobotka. There was a small Christmas celebration, but no festive mood. The temperature had fallen by then to minus 38° (-36° F). We spent the freezing night in the shed of a collective farm that had lost its roof. But at least we were glad to be surrounded by walls that protected us somewhat from the piercing wind. I had covered myself with a thick woolen blanket, and fine, glistening snow fell lightly on us continuously...

On January 2, 1943, our battery was transferred to Mamonovo, 25 kilometers from Slobotka, and on the 28th, even deeper in the snow hell, to Usochi, near Bol Scheltuchi. As a nineteen year old driver, I had then

27

Our strenuous march with the heavy equipment, through the hell of the Russian winter.

to take my horse-drawn observation cart or sled right up to the area of the front. From a distance, the thunder of the cannon at the front sounded like a dull, rolling boil. But worse was the fact that supplies for our soldiers, as well as hay and straw for the horses, had to be transported from the railhead closest to our position almost every day. Each way was 40 kilometers long; thus we had to manage a trip of 80 kilometers a day through a hell of snow and ice, in temperatures that had fallen to minus 48° C (-54° F). Since there was merely a narrow corduroy road through the often head-high snow, one couldn't walk next to the sled, but had to remain seated on it the whole time, and so had no chance to move about. The animals screamed from fear, pain and fatigue and often had to struggle to keep moving forward. After each one of these trips the horses were shot by the veterinary - they were completely done in by this grueling trip... *(For me, a farmer's son, to live through this every day was exceptionally brutal, as I had a special feeling for these animals.)*

When we came back in the evening, there was lukewarm soup waiting for us. As a result of the severe supply problems there was, for example, only sauerkraut soup for an entire week, usually with a small piece of ground-up meat of the horse that had earlier struggled through the winter hell with me... Rations in Russia were extremely bad. We were com-

28

Horse-drawn sled at minus 48° centigrade - 80 kilometers daily...

pletely undernourished, which in the Russian cold, and with the unusual exertions was, naturally, particularly harmful. In addition, there was often frostbite, particularly on the hands and feet, but it also happened that someone lost his ears or nose to frostbite.

On January 20, 1943, I noticed that all the toes of both my feet were frozen. Three days later, the nails of the big toes had fallen off, and in turn, the nails of the next ones, and the flesh could be pushed to the side or squeezed out of shape without returning to its original form. In the meantime, it began to have an extremely disagreeable smell, as the dead flesh began to decompose.

When I reported in sick to the infirmary with my frostbite, I happened to be treated by an unusually understanding major, who said:

"Young fellow, under no circumstances must you go to the base hospital. Because anyone who goes to the base hospital with frostbite is court-martialed for self-mutilation. For that, the sentence can be death..."

So I had, somehow, to get over the frostbite by myself, and there was a danger that the toes would have to be amputated. I was relieved from normal duty for the time being and, with only woven straw shoes on my feet, I sharpened spades in the ordnance shop with a file. During the two weeks I did that work, my toes returned to normal. I was unusually lucky to have been able to keep my toes after frostbite.

Because of the frostbite, I became a little cautious when it came to cold. One day - it was on Sunday, the 4th of March - we stood in the snow with the temperature at minus 30° C (-22° F), and shivered. Since our cook had trouble getting up in the morning, we often had to wait for a long time - freezing - to get our breakfast coffee. I already knew that, and so, as always, had gone later, and I was annoyed to have to wait in spite of that. So I expressed my unhappiness with plain words, which did not at all please our lazy "kitchen bully". He reported it to the top-kick and he reported it to the battery commander,, 1st Lt. Wilkening. He, in turn, had me do the *Kaiser-Wilhelm-Memorial-March* twice for half an hour. That is, I had to do exercises in the snow and cold as punishment, while wearing a gas mask. The pleasure of meting out my punishment was given to a "Wachtmeister" of our company. *(Wachtmeister, in the cavalry and horse artillery, corresponding to Feldwebel in the infantry, was a grade equivalent to a Staff Sergeant in the U.S. Army. Functionally, the Wacht-meister was the company sergeant major, or first sergeant.)* And with the whole running about, the ups and downs, the exertions under the extremely harsh conditions of the Russian winter, he managed to have me completely "done in" in the first half hour. *(He was killed only a couple of weeks later - which did not overly sadden me, as I would suffer from then on, for the rest of my life, from asthma and bronchitis.)*

In the following days my health deteriorated, I had fever, a sore throat and trouble breathing. When, on March 13th, it was time for me to be inoculated along with the other soldiers I was already feeling very bad. The medical officer was shocked:

"My God, what do you have now...?"

After the medic had taken my temperature he said it had already risen to over 40° C (104° F). The medical officer ordered on the spot:

"Put him to bed immediately!"

I didn't even have a chance to get my things from my quarters.

On the next day I was taken to the clearing station in Bol Scheltuchi, and since my condition didn't improve, I was taken to the division hospital in Mokroje two days later. During that time I had hallucinations. I was given an injection to lower my fever, but the medic must have made some kind of error, for after that my condition worsened dramatically.

I lay under a number of thick woolen blankets, but I felt my feet slowly becoming cold. The cold crept further and further up my body, and as it reached my thighs, my hands also began to get cold. I could sense it all clearly. When, however, I tried to speak, it was no longer possible - everything became dark around me...

(Later, a wounded patient in the bed next to me told me he had noticed that something was not right with me; suddenly I showed no signs of life. So he called a medical sergeant who revived me with a vigorous cardiac massage. My heart must have beat slower and slower, and shortly before, stopped completely...)

Two days later, on March 18th, I was taken from Mokroje to Bedlitza and from there through snow and ice on a self-propelled assault gun to Base Hospital 664 in Roslavl, where I arrived the next day. There I was diagnosed with chronic tonsillitis, and an emergency operation was scheduled. But there were many reasons why this operation might not be possible. The hospital was hopelessly overcrowded with sick and wounded - the soldiers were even lying crowded on the floor. It also caught my eye that there were half-starved and completely bedraggled sailors of a U-Boat crew who belonged to a penal command. They were said to have mutinied. As I learned, they had been sent directly in front of the lines and, without weapons, had been put to work laying or clearing mines - on the white snow, in their conspicuous dark-blue naval uniforms...

And since the Russians kept pressure on the front daily, and I would have to stay in bed longer after the operation, the doctors procrastinated in my case. They wanted to wait a little longer. So the days went by. I was bedridden the entire time, but had to wear my uniform, since the armored and dreaded Russian slow, low flying planes *(they were called "sewing machines" on account of the sound of their motors)* came more and more often at night and dropped fragmentation bombs, even on our hospital. And so it happened often that, despite illness or wounds, we had to take cover in the snowy slit trenches. The suffering of the men was almost indescribable. And so it went for all of April.

When the swelling in my throat from the tonsillitis had become so severe that it was apparent it could not be operated on in this hospital, I was sent, as a precaution, to Warsaw, to Medical Collection Station II, which was set up in a hotel on the Weichselbrücke. When I arrived there my legs and feet were so swollen from the strain on my heart *(congestive heart failure)* that I could no longer get my boots off.

In this medical collection station, all the wounded and ill were asked if they could endure a further transport. Even though I was really in bad shape, when I heard that the further transport would be to Germany, I declared myself fit for transport.

On May 5[th,] we started out in the direction of our homeland, and after

31

a rail trip of three days and nights, I finally arrived at the Reserve Hospital in Armsdorf, near Dresden. The operation for which I was sent back home was, however delayed further. On the 14th my mother visited me, but she hadn't recognized me because my face and neck were so swollen and distorted. On the next day, finally, I had the operation - after six weeks.

I stayed in the hospital another four weeks, and then, on June 23rd, my mother visited me for a second time. It was my birthday, and I was recovering. I received a 14-day recuperation leave and went home with my mother to our hometown, Metzingen.

The winter service in Russia and my severe illness had stamped not only my face...

My recuperation leave went by much too swiftly. On July 9th I reported to the convalescent battery of Replacement Battalion 31, in Rautheim, near Brunswick, in the Heinrich-der-Löwe-Barracks, and had the great good luck on the 11th to get a further 14-day leave. Since the end of this leave fell during the harvest season I, as the son of a farmer, received another three weeks of harvest leave - by telegram.

On August 12th I had to report back to the barracks in Brunswick. Each soldier's leaves were entered in his pay book. But my pay book had been lost during my transport from Russia to Germany *(during the time of my illness and occasional mental lapses)*. Then I got a substitute pay book. All my personal data was appended. When I was finally recovered, I was sent to a non-commissioned officers' training course in Brunswick. The plan was that I was to be transferred after that to the

Riviera as a non-commissioned officer, as a cure for my asthma, and to serve as an instructor.

During this non-commissioned officer training course in horse-drawn transportation at the Hindenburg Barracks in Brunswick, my father visited me one day. He asked me if I had met one Hein Meinheit. I had no idea whom he meant, and he explained to me that Meinheit was a mayor *(like my father)* from the town of Oldau in the Lueneburger Heath.

"Well, and what is with him?", I asked.

"I have just seen him here in the barracks", he replied, "and I asked him to get you a team of horses with which to forage for supplies."

He explained to me that Corporal Meinheit was a forager, in addition to which he "greased" all his superiors with sausage spread and ham, so as to become indispensable *(although he was only responsible for twenty horses)* and to be able to stay in the homeland. *(As a farmer, he had no lack of the produce needed to trade for these supplies.)* Hein Meinhart would see me soon about the team of horses.

A few days later the forager contacted me himself. He appeared jolly, and talked with me for a time. Then he said to me with a confidential smile:

"I have a girlfriend for you, young fellow..."

I put him off immediately:

"Oh no, as long as the war goes on I don't want to have a girlfriend. I had one, and when it came time for me to go to Russia I broke up with her. It is better that way..."

After only a few more days had passed, I was lying on my bed in our quarters when the duty non-com whistled for me and called down the floor:

"Private Severloh report to room 53!"

That was, as I soon found out, Hein Meinheit's room. He had actually already been a soldier for two or three years, had never loaded a rifle, and instead only concerned himself with his horses; his object was simply not ever to leave home. He still wore his own clothes, even to his boots, and he "greased" everyone; whether captain or major, they were all "dependent". Butter, eggs, sausage and ham were the best currency in these difficult times, and so he made himself essential.

There was also a captain there named Schliephake, who was liaison officer between the army and the farmers *(purchase of horses, fodder, etc.)*. This captain had a 19 year-old daughter who practiced riding at the barracks and, as a consequence, was frequently there. Now I had to report to Room 53, to Corporal Meinheit. When I entered, two young girls were sitting there and smiled at me. One of the two was the daughter of the captain; her name was Elisabeth. Meinheit whispered to me:

"That is really something for you..."

Elisabeth Schliephake with her horse, Rosa, at the front door of her parents' manor house in Rautheim, in 1943.

It turned out that Lisa, as I later called her, was not only the daughter of the captain, but also the daughter of the largest farmer of the nearby community of Rautheim, only one kilometer distant. During the next two weeks Lisa and I met another five or six times, and were very attracted to each other.

Then I learned that during my absence, the division to which my old unit belonged, the 321st Infantry Division, had been transferred from Russia - where, in the meantime, it had sustained crippling losses - to France, in Normandy, and reorganized. *(Only the 1st Battery had stayed in Russia, as it was the only one still intact.)*

So I was again assigned to a replacement battalion, and arrived at the Mars-la-Tour-Barracks in Brunswick. Naturally, I resisted being sent back to my old unit, but nothing worked, and the non-com training was terminated. Since the climate in Normandy, strongly influenced by the Gulf Stream, is very healthy, the old plan of sending me to the warm

34

Mediterranean as an instructor was abandoned - and a week later I was already on the train to northern France, rather than to the Riviera.

Then on December 11[th,] I rejoined my old unit, which, in the meantime, had been renamed the 352nd Infantry Division, and was located at St.-Michel-de-la-Pierre, south of St. Lô, in Normandy. The rest of the two batteries were re-supplied there during the following days with soldiers, horses, materiel and weapons, and three new batteries were created as part of Artillery Regiment 352.

At first, in St. Aubin, near Calais, we had a really likeable battery clerk named Kopius, but he was discharged only eight weeks later. The new one had been a dairyman in civilian life, couldn't stand farmers, portrayed them as the epitome of stupidity, and had a big, foul mouth: August Wassermeier. His favorite invectives were terms for "stable muckers" and for "cribbers" (horses who sucked air when eating, and bit the rim of the feeding trough). He generally ended every formation by shouting:

"Feeding is over; Attention! Dismissed!"

In every battery there were two categories of soldiers: some were cannoneers (the crew for the gun), the others were the teamsters (responsible for the vehicles and the horses). There were always disputes between the two camps, and continuous friction ("damned cannoneers" and "damned Teamsters"). At that time I was assigned as a teamster, Wassermeier was a cannoneer, and this circumstance didn't do anything to improve our relationship...

When I joined the 352nd Infantry Division in Normandy - after 13 weeks leave and a total of 9 long month's absence from my unit - and reported to the orderly room in St.-Michel-de-la-Pierre, I saw that the "top-kick" was still the same: August Wassermeier, the dairyman...

"Gimme your pay book!", he ordered curtly.

I gave it to him

"I think something's missing..."

"This is, after all, my replacement pay book", I explained, although that was quite clear to see.

He was annoyed, and snorted:

"No war can last long enough for you ever to get another leave!"

That was the moment when my attitude changed and I became obstinate. Of course, it wasn't great to sit around at home after the war had begun, while everyone else had become a soldier, whether voluntarily, or not, as in my case. But what disturbed me the most was this

35

"slavish submission"; it was always:

"Shut up when you are talking with me! And leave the thinking to the horses; they have bigger heads!"

You always had to abase yourself, to cower, to subordinate yourself to the stupidest superior. Human relations and psychology were concepts that didn't seem to be understood. A soldier who believed he should think for himself would often be tormented for so long that the last shred of initiative would be gone. That had also been my experience up until now, when I arrived in Normandy. I had to, and wanted, now, to go my own way, and from now on was only going to think about how to work things out to my own best advantage, bearing in mind what the doctor (major) in Brunswick had said after reviewing my medical records. I was no longer, as it happened, *fit for active duty*, but *fit only for limited duty in the homeland*. Now, however, this cursed division had been transferred to Normandy and I had been forced to follow it there instead of going to the Riviera. I resolved never again to march one step - never again...!

It is true that, as the tallest in our battery, I was again the flank man and had, therefore, to march at the head of the column, but I always was the last to fall in. Whenever someone gave me the order to move out, I answered with the most ingenuous expression I could manage:

"I am not allowed to; the doctor in charge has forbidden it."

One day, however, it was too much for the battery clerk, and the dairyman barked at me:

"Get over to the medics right now to be examined!"

When I reported to the doctor (a captain) I had to undress, and he listened to my chest. Then he read my medical record that had come along to the Division along with my other records, and asked:

"To what position are you assigned?"

"Mounted messenger", I answered.

"You really like to work with horses?"

"Yes", I lied, for the fact was that working with the horses was a real grind.

But he shook his head:

"No more riding on a horse; you also can't perform any infantry duties and also no running..."

Now the sun rose for me, and I thought:

August Wassermeier, that was it; from now on there is nothing you can do to me...

After that I always fell into formation as flank man too late. Later,

I was billeted in the house right next to the roll-call area - but I was still always the last to arrive...

Then I received an unexpected Christmas present when, on December 25th, I was assigned to the newly deployed 1st Battery in the small hamlet of St. Martin. Wassermeier sent all his "barn muckers" and "unsound horses" to this unit. I also left along with the others. Now I was finally free of August Wassermeier and our old battery commander, 1st Lt. Wilkening.

Our new battery clerk was First Sergeant Uwe Karsten. He was a good fellow. He liked me and took me aside on December 28th, saying:

"Look here, Hein, we are getting a new commander today, and it occurred to us that you should become his 'orderly'..."

Smiling, Karsten added:

"But I want to tell you one thing. When you are the battery commander's orderly, and he knows something, you have only one hour - and then I am to know it, too..."

Then he got serious again, and said:

"You can sometimes take your time coming to formations..."

That caught my attention: Formation? You can take your time...? No, I cannot! After that I quit going to any formations, since as orderly to the battery commander I had, so to speak, a privileged position... *(except on April 20th, Hitler's birthday)*.

In the evening there was a formation of the battery complement *(the last one for me)*. The new commander introduced himself and shook hands with each man *(he hardly knew any of us, for it was a newly formed unit)*. I was the flank man and stood in the third, rear rank. 1st Lt. Frerking stopped in front of me, and looked me in the eyes - and we took to each other from the first moment on. He didn't yet know that I had been assigned as his orderly...

Frerking was an upper school teacher of English, French and Sports, 32 years old, who also had come from Russia, and was a real combat soldier (along the lines of Bill Mauldin's "Willie and Joe"). He had been decorated with the Iron Cross, 2nd Class and a "Frozen Flesh Order" *(the medal for participation in the Russian Winter Campaign of 1941/42)*.

Our new commander showed himself early-on to be an intelligent commander who would become extremely popular with his troops. In any case, I was already relieved officially - with a medical certificate - from marching and riding. Only a couple of people who knew me had come with me to the new 1st Battery from the 3rd Battery, and respected

Photo on the page to the left: My new battery commander, 1ˢᵗ Lt. Bernhard Frerking (left, and in the small photo), together with Master Sgt. Ludwig Meyer who was, after our transfer to Normandy our new "top-kick".

me because they had been entertained by the way I always set August Wassermeier's teeth on edge; they were the "top-kick", Uwe Karsten, as well as several sergeants and a technical sergeant.

On January 4, 1944, our unit was transferred to the nearby village of Mojon, near the regimental headquarters in St. Samson. A large room in one of the old houses of this village was used as a barracks and I was assigned there along with ten other soldiers. As the ranking private of our detail I had first choice of a sleeping place. I arranged a straw bed there on the floor. Then I had a visit from a good buddy whom I had already met in Brunswick, and with whom I had been sent to Normandy. He was tipsy, and told me that he had drunk an awesome French liquor that packed a terrific punch...

I asked, "How much of it did you drink?"

"Three", he answered

I said, shaking my head,

"There's no liquor that can make you drunk after only three shots. What is this stuff called?"

"Don't know, it had such a funny name..."

I really tried to lay it on him:

"Look, you can always drink ten before you really feel anything..."

"Good", he said, "if you can drink ten shots of the stuff and still stand up on the table on one leg, then I'll pay for the ten. If you can't, you pay."

I agreed.

Then we went to a café, and I ordered ten shots of the liquor. I hadn't taken into account that I had only eaten a small, lightly buttered piece of bread after the long march to St. Samson that day. Then I explained to the Mademoiselle that I didn't want the drinks one after the other, but lined up in a row. She looked at me with something between astonishment and sympathy, then served up the full ten shots. I took the first one and knocked it back. I realized immediately that this must be a particularly wicked drink, and thought for a moment that I would go up in flames on the spot. It was clear to me right away that I would have to hurry up the drinking if I wanted to win my bet; I would have to drink the booze before its ruinous effect could set in. Within a minute, with tears in my eyes, I had drunk the other nine shots, jumped up on the table, stood on one leg,

39

and won my bet.

Meanwhile, four other comrades had come in, and each of us bought another round of this devil's brew, whose name I now learned:

"Galvadosch", I babbled to myself, as I left the café by myself with my rifle under my arm to look for my quarters, just as darkness was falling. But the way there was not so simple...

A Frenchman had left his team in front of the café, and with the 16 Calvados in my blood, at first I walked toward the bulky grey horses. After I bounced off the horses I looked for the right direction. The road forked across from the café, and I had come here on one of the two... I gathered all my drunken wits and remembered that I had about four hundred meters to go from the café. If I took the wrong road, I would have to know it after four hundred meters, and return, in order to take the other one. I staggered off, but walking upright became an increasing problem, and my body kept succumbing to the gravitational pull of the earth...*(It must have been a bizarre picture, as I crept back to my quarters in riding britches and riding boots, with my rifle dragging behind me. The road I had chosen was actually the right one, but it took me a whole hour to navigate it...)*

In my drunken state I walked right into the horse of one of these farm carts typical of the area. It was in this sort of "charrette" (= carriage) that I often drove Lt. Frerking around.

40

On February 11[th.] we deployed, as ordered, from the eastern coast of the Cotentin Peninsula to the coast of Grandcamp - to the "Atlantic Watch". It was a long march of almost 70 kilometers. We were on the way for three days and had to bivouac for two nights. *(This shift of the entire 352nd Infantry Division is said to have remained unknown to the Allies, despite their dense spy network, and later was the cause of the American tragedy at "Omaha"...)*

On the evening of our first overnight stop, five other officers of the unit presented themselves at my new commander's quarters. Lt. Frerking said:

"Severloh, we would like to drink a cognac..."

He gave me some money and I bought a bottle of cognac in the small village nearby. But we had no glasses, and the thought of drinking good cognac from cups or canteen cups was unpleasant. So Frerking assigned me the task of getting glasses as well.

It was still light as I walked through the small village looking for a store where I could buy some glasses, but I didn't find one. There wasn't a single bar in this village. At some point I simply went into a house. The front door was unlocked, and the large room that was entered directly from the street was entry, kitchen and living room all in one. I had never seen such an odd room. In the middle of the room, on an oval tray on a table, there were six glasses - exactly the number needed for tonight. With their elongated shape and thick bottoms they would do well for highballs, whiskey, calvados or our cognac. But there was no one besides me in this unusual room. To make my presence known I said loudly:

"Bonjour"

I waited for a moment, but no one reacted, and I said again, and louder:

"Bonjour!"

Again nothing, upon which I shouted my French greeting three more times. But clearly I was alone in this house. By my fifth shouted greeting I had already unbuttoned the two top buttons of my jacket. Then I put three glasses in on the left and three on the right, and called out *(no longer quite so loud)*:

"Au revoir!", and I was again outside.

(At that time I saw my deal as a prank. All that mattered to me was to succeed for my commander in returning to his quarters with six beautiful glasses. Today I would like to go to that house to pay the owner for his glasses, and explain to him where they went so suddenly back then, but

unfortunately, I don't even remember the name of the small hamlet.)

That evening I served the cognac in the six glasses on a pretty tray and proudly carried them into the comfortable living room. 1st Lt. Frerking was delighted. But later, when the other officers had left, he said to me:

"I really liked the glasses, Severloh, but where did you get them?"

I was surprised, not having counted on that question, and having kept the money. On the spur of the moment I lied:

"Over there, from the little store next to the church..."

The lieutenant came right up to me and looked me deep and seriously in the eyes:

"Once more, Severloh, and I will have you locked up for as long as this war lasts..."

I was completely nonplussed, and looked down at the toes of my boots. Frerking continued:

"There is no church at all in this village..."

(Later we often laughed about the small matter of the six pilfered glasses.)

On February 14^{th,} our 1st Battery moved into position near the small hamlet of Houtteville. It was about eight kilometers northwest of Bayeux and some four-and-a-half kilometers distant from the coast. First Lieutenant Frerking and I had the good luck to be quartered at the large and lovely manor house of the friendly Legrand family. *(By this time the Chief of Staff to the Supreme Allied Commander - COSSAC - located in England had already chosen the coastal strip of our artillery target area as part of one of the two American landing areas, "Utah" and "Omaha". Our target area was in "Easy Red" sector of Omaha Beach.)*

A German artillery unit was composed of one battery (corresponding to a company in the infantry), and three to four batteries constituted an "Abteilung", corresponding to an infantry battalion. Normally a battery consisted of four guns - cannon, howitzers or large caliber mortars. A battery had a limber park area, an orderly room, an observation post and a firing position. In our case the limber park area lay in the small village of Mandeville, about eight kilometers from the coast, our orderly room was in a chateau in l'Epinette, almost halfway to our firing position near tiny Houtteville, further north. The battery commander (1st Lt. Frerking) was also stationed there, although his only combat station as commander was the observation post on the front line, in the event of an

The chateau of l'Epinette, ten kilometers from the coast, where the battery office was located, which we soldiers referred to merely as the orderly room.

attack on the beach. This observation post was on the coastal heights in front of the hamlet of Colleville, in Strongpoint WN 62.

The crew of a howitzer consisted of the section chief (corporal) and five troops (one gunner and four cannoneers). The usual crew of the observation post consisted of seven persons, including, in case of an alert, Lt. Frerking - and me as his bodygard...

Our battery commander was positioned behind a telescope with a built-in scale for observing the targets and the fall of the shells, so as to be able to correct the firing settings as necessary. The firing orders were transmitted from the observation post by telephone or radio, to the battery. The section chiefs adjusted their sights accordingly and gave the command to fire when ordered. Every battery had a so-called calculator, who computed the coordinates for the section chief. All data relayed from the O.P. (observation post) had to be factored in, and was called a "Barba" message, which was updated every morning. For example, the wind direction, the wind speed and the temperature. The order "more" meant a slight turn to the right. "Top" meant the elevation adjustment of the barrel, and was based on the distance the shell had to travel to the target (ballistics). The target locations had been previously determined, since the guns could not be fired without destroying the beach obstacles. Practice rounds were simply fired from a position 300 meters forward, and then the guns were returned to their basic positions. The last practice rounds fired toward the beach were eight days before the invasion.

Gun crew of the first gun of the 1st Battery, 1st Abteilung of the 352nd Artillery Regiment in the firing position near Houtteville, in May, 1944. Section Chief: Sgt. Richard Peesel (2nd from left).

The relationship with the owners of the estate at which we had been quartered grew into a very pleasant one. The nearly 50 year-old Monsieur Fernand Legrand had, himself, been a 1st Lieutenant of artillery in the First World War and, coincidentally, in a 105 mm howitzer battery. He asked me occasionally if Lt. Frerking had plans for the evening, and otherwise he would invite him to take a calvados with him. Since, however, I also wanted to join in, I would say to my chief:

"Herr Oberleutnant, *we* are invited to join Monsieur Legrand in the kitchen this evening for a drink of calvados..."

So Monsieur Legrand would have to put out another glass for me. But he liked me, and we often had a stimulating conversation. There was no problem communicating, since Frerking, a French teacher, had a fluent command of the language, and I caught on to the language very well.

When we would sit for a long time in the evening with Legrand, and

Firing of one of the four howitzers of our 1ˢᵗ Battery, in the firing position under the tall trees near Houtteville, On the horizon, the Legrand manor house, over which the gun fired at "Omaha Beach", four and one half kilometers distant.

the fire in the open fireplace died down, he would throw a shot of calvados on it; a fireball would puff up from the embers and the flames of the fire would blaze up again.

Once I was talking to Monsieur Legrand alone. He owned a beautiful hunting dog. I asked Legrand how old the dog was. He answered:

"Three years."

"Can he already retrieve?", I inquired further. Legrand said he could.

If the dog was three years old and was a retriever, something must have been shot that he could have retrieved... I concluded from this that Monsieur Legrand must have a firearm *(which had been strictly forbidden since the German occupation of France in 1940).* I knew intuitively, however, that he never would have turned it on us. So I kept this knowledge to myself and said nothing of it to Lt. Frerking...

The Legrands and I very soon developed a remarkable agreeable relationship. My conversations with Madame Legrand, who also spoke some Polish and German, were mostly in a mixture of the three languages. *(I could also speak a little French and some Polish),* and no one who overheard our unusual conversation could understand what we were talking about. *We* understood each other wonderfully...

Monsieur Fernand Legrand in front of his luxurious Citro - a man of quality.

Personally, I had a generally good relationship with the French people of the village, and believe I can say that I was *(despite my German uniform)* genuinely well liked. Occasionally, I would go through the village and buy an egg, sometimes from one farmer and sometimes from another. But always only one. Actually I supplied myself and my chief with eggs mainly from Legrand's large henhouse... If Monsieur Legrand had ever formed a suspicion I would have been able to name the whole bunch of people who would be able to confirm truthfully that I had bought our eggs from them quite legally...

At this point I have to note that the relationship between the French, and the German troops (insofar as I could judge from my observations and experiences in Normandy) could be described as rather good. In many aspects of daily life there was a very positive willingness to co-operate on both sides. For instance, in working the farmland. Many French farmers were still prisoners-of-war in Germany, and horses were rare on the farms. So, many German soldiers, with their horses, were ordered to help with the cultivation of the fields and other work on the properties.

Over time, Lt. Frerking and I developed a really friendly relationship. I liked and respected my chief for his genuine human qualities, and he liked my sly and mischievous nature. Frerking was an extremely correct person, but once we had a quarrel about a horse that had, for two days, had no feed, and had to pull our "charrette". Although 1st Lt. Frerking knew about that, he ordered me to urge the horse on, but I refused. We had a serious quarrel about it, and in my anger I used heated words to tell my superior what I thought of such cruelty to an animal. Frerking accommodated to my attitude. It also appeared to me over time that Frerking's family at home was having a hard time. Since I made purchases for him, I was aware that he sent home as much as he possibly could for his wife and two children.

I knew my chief was fond of me, and he often smiled when he found out about my little pranks. Laughing mischievously, he often called me Till *(on account of my sly mischievousness, alluding to Till Eulenspiegel)*. Moreover, we both listened to the strictly-forbidden "*Soldiers' Broadcast Station, Calais*". When I was not in the house, Frerking listened to the broadcast; when *he* was not there, I listened. A couple of times we caught each other at it. Neither of us said anything about it...

One of the broadcasts that could be heard on this German language BBC propaganda station stuck in my memory. The speaker mixed up the biblical saying, "Love they neighbor as thyself" and the saying "Strike while the iron is hot" to "Strike yourself like the iron and love your neighbor as long as he is hot"...

In May 1944, it was unusually warm. The Aure River, which ran not far from the Legrand estate, had been dammed on Rommel's orders *(to prevent the extension of any enemy landing of airborne troops in this part of the close inland area of the coast).* The water temperature of the flooded meadows was a good 20° (68° F) and I would have liked to go swimming, but had, however, to attend to my duties. I thought about how I could change this...

On one of the following mornings, a tradesman came to Legrand's courtyard with a horse and wagon, and offered Madame Legrand some snails. I saw that she had bought a large amount. So I went to Frerking right away, and said:

"Herr Oberleutnant", Madame Legrand is probably going to ask if you would come down to lunch today - there are snails..."

Frerking reacted, as I had hoped:

"For Heaven's sake! Go quickly and tell Schorse to bring the horses, I have to leave right away..."

Shortly after he had left, I went swimming...

One day, after Pentecost, after the officers of the Ist Detachment of Artillery Regiment 352 had put on a hunt near St. Lô, several of these officers came to Frerking's quarters in the evening. Major Pluskat, commander of our Ist Battalion, Captain Wilkening of the 3rd Battery *(who had had me tormented so barbarously in Russia)*, the commander of the 2nd, and four other 1st Lieutenants; there was a total of eight. The day's hunt was discussed, among other things. *(It was customary, on a hunt, that the ranking officer rode at the front, and all the others followed him, in the order of their rank. There was an artillery tradition that all officers rode. Many of them weren't able to do much more than sit their horses, but nevertheless, all had to ride.)*

Before I put the glasses on the table, Lt. Frerking whispered to me:

"Severloh, we have to get the major and the captain drunk after a while..."

"How shall I manage that?", I asked.

"That's up to you", he replied, and left me standing there.

I had several bottles of cognac and a couple of bottles of calvados.

Well, I began to serve; always precisely according to rank. I started with Pluskat - with the extra-strong calvados. Then I served Captain Wilkening, and the bottle was *(as intended)* empty. I upended the bottle a bit so that they all could see that it really was empty and there was nothing left in it. Then I took the decidedly milder cognac and continued serving. Pretty soon the major and the captain no longer noticed that only they got the strong calvados *(from a different bottle)*.

Gathering of the officers for a hunt. In the middle of the photo, the com-
mander of our 1st Abteilung, Major Werner Pluskat. (Far left, my battery
commander, 1st Lieutenant Bernhard Frerking.) In a long address on
June 2, 1944, Pluskat gave us to understand, indirectly, that when the
expected invasion occurred we should decamp quickly if possible. But
why...? He, himself, was not with his unit on the day of the invasion.
Pluskat's situation in the 1961 film, "The Longest Day" was not truthfully
portrayed. During the attack of June 6th, Lt. Frerking had tried repea-
tedly to contact him by telephone - but our abteilung commander was
nowhere to be found...

When, finally, the two ranking officers had become so completely
drunk that the others could slip into an adjoining room, they got a jeep to
take them to the girls at the front-theatre in Trévières, only ten kilometers
away - there were only six women at this theatre...

On June 5th, *(one day before the invasion - the weather cold and rainy)*
I played my last practical joke. I sat in the courtyard in front of Legrand's
house and, out of boredom, cleaned my rifle. When I was finished, it
occurred to me to irritate the gunners a bit. If you knew where it was, and
had sharp eyes, you could see the well-camouflaged gun that stood about
four hundred meters from the manor house. First I considered whether I

should shoot at one of the large, steel gun shields. I knew there would be a very loud reverberation when the bullet hit it. But then I had scruples, fearing that the shot might hit someone. So I looked for a different target. A fir tree about ten meters high and at some distance from the entrance to Legrand's property caught my eye. I aimed, targeting the approximately 15 centimeter thick trunk, and fired. A couple of light colored splinters flew off, and when I looked at the tree afterwards, it had a small entry hole in front, and was thoroughly split at the back. *(What I had really done with my frivolous shot, I would only learn many years later...)*

In the Hell of Omaha

At 0055 hours we arrived at the strongpoint in our little charrette. We had, in fact, taken the shortest route to Widerstandsnest 62 *(the coastal defenses of Omaha Beach consisted of a series of strongpoints known as Widerstandsnests).* We had taken the road from Saint Laurent and along the bluff line, though we had left ourselves plenty of time, and had driven through the dark night at a leisurely pace. We were sure that no attack would come before daylight. From a distance, to the west, the motors of large aircraft droned without interruption. *(I only learned later about the American airborne landing that took place at that time in the area of Sainte-Mère-Église, almost forty kilometers distant...)*

The landing beach named "Omaha" by the Allies, with the three sectors, "Dog", "Easy" and "Fox", was of such great interest to them because there were three roads and three other narrow routes that led from the beach to the interior through the cuts in the coastal bluff. These roads were very important for a rapid advance of allied troops, and their supply. The two approaches leading to Vierville and St. Laurent were blocked with concrete barriers over two meters high, the one leading to Colleville mined "only" in some sections, and heavily barricaded with barbed wire, as well as obstacles.
From Ste.-Honorine-des-Pertes, through St. Laurent, to Vierville there were a total of 15 strongpoints (from Widerstandsnest 59 to 73), and on the broad bay there were five artillery pieces installed in reinforced concrete casemates, and several in improvised positions. Oddly enough, there was not a single heavy anti-aircraft gun in any of the fortifications. There were about three hundred sixty German soldiers stationed in the

15 strongpoints, with a total of 65 machine guns. Since Field Marshal Rommel had recognized that the strategically most important area in the entire bay ("Omaha") was the break in the bluffs in front of Colleville - with its road - three strongpoints were built in this area alone, with the following installations:

WN 60, with a 20-mm anti-aircraft gun, three 50-mm mortars, one Renault tank turret with a 50-mm gun, two defensive flame throwers and an artillery observation post; WN 61, with one 88-mm gun in a fortified casemate, one Renault tank turret with a 50-mm gun, one 50-mm anti-tank gun, two Tobruk positions for machine guns, an artillery observation post, and two flame throwers; WN 62, with two 76.5-mm guns in fortified casemates, two 50-mm anti-tank guns, two 50-mm mortars, and two water-cooled Polish machine guns, all in earthen bunkers, one twin MG-34 machine gun for anti-aircraft defense, one MG 34 machine gun and one MG 42 machine gun, in open positions, an artillery observation post, as well as two defensive flame throwers, and in front, an anti-tank ditch about 300 meters long.

Around all the strongpoints there were heavily mined areas, and they were protected by thick, sometimes multi-row barriers of barbed wire. The entire beach was barricaded with hundreds of large and small obstacles (steel "Czech Hedgehogs", "Belgian Gates", ramp racks and tree trunks tipped with mines as well as many thousands of mines).

WN 62 represented the strongest position in the entire bay, and had a permanent complement of 27 soldiers of the 3rd Company of Grenadier Regiment 726 of the 716th Infantry Division. The observation post and communications position of our 1st Battery was located in this Widerstandsnest (about one-third of the way up and at a height of about twenty meters, on the limestone terrain of the strongpoint that rose at an angle of about 20° to a height of almost 50 meters). They were always manned by seven soldiers of our unit: Lieutenant Grass, Technical Sgt. Fack, Sgt. Beermann, as well as Pfc's Wernecke and Schulz, and two radio operators. Lt. Frerking (and I) were only required to be present in the event of an attack. As Battery Commander, he had to observe and direct the artillery fire of our battery from the observation post. A machine gun seven meters to the side of the observation post bunker was in position for me at all times, at the end of the communication trench.

The central command (battalion command post) of the 716th Infantry Division was in the large, half-underground bunker, WN 63, that lay 1,340 meters to the rear, on the road from the beach to Colleville, just

short of the village and not far from the church. The battalion comman-
der was Major Dr. Ernst-August Lohmann.

When we arrived at WN 62, Sgt. Beermann was already waiting for us, and took over the team to take it back to a stable in Colleville. After our arrival the only entrance to the strongpoint was barricaded with barbed wire and mines by a soldier of Grenadier Regiment 726 *(so that it could not be taken easily from the rear in the event it was surrounded by the enemy).* In the darkness, the trenches and bunkers were only dimly visible; the garrison couldn't be seen, as the soldiers were all at their posts in their bunkers or positions. Lt. Frerking went immediately to his small observation post bunker; it held only three people and had been hardened with reinforced concrete only that spring. I went to my machine gun position. The ammunition had already been put out and the machine gun, as always, positioned. *(The modern machine gun, Model 1942, achieved a markedly higher rate of fire than the previous 1934 model and because of that it was also referred to, sarcastically, as Hitler's Buzz Saw or Hitler's Zipper...)*

After I had loaded the first ammunition belt and readied my machine gun for firing, I climbed back out of my machine gun position, stood on the roof of the observation post, and peered through the darkness at the sea. Dawn had just started to break, but it was still more dark than light when I noticed five or six large, dark silhouettes of ships more than ten kilometers distant out on the sea. I called to Lt. Frerking to come up from the bunker, and Lt. Grass followed him up to where I was standing. But just at that moment the ships disappeared again *(I learned only later that, as dawn was breaking, the allied fleet laid down a smoke screen).* Although Lt. Frerking said he could still see the ships, I doubted it. I advised him that he might want to call our commander, Major Pluskat, at battalion headquarters. After a little while Frerking came back up and said he hadn't been able to reach the major either at his quarters in the chateau at Etréham, at the battalion headquarters, or at the battalion command post: Pluskat was simply not there... At that, I remarked half aloud:

"Probably he's taking the girls of the front-theatre back to Paris just now..."

Frerking looked at me out of the corner of his eye and smiled in a manner that said a lot, then he phoned to the naval artillery strongpoint at the small fishing port of Port-en-Bessin, seven kilometers away. Shortly thereafter, the naval artillery fired two red, and two green signal flares, to try to learn if the ships were perhaps German warships. But from the ships in the smoke came no answer...

After the man-made smoke had cleared, we caught sight of the largest armada of all time - a sight as frightening as it was awesome.

Toward 0500 hours *(it had become light in the meantime, but the sea and the sky both appeared blue-grey in the hazy light coming through the clouds)* the smoke parted suddenly on the horizon and revealed the view of the most powerful armada in history. Across the entire horizon stretched an endless, uninterrupted band of ships, some of which were enormous. *(On these ships, 34,142 American soldiers approached their target area, "Omaha", along with 3,306 tanks and military vehicles. I didn't know at that time that there were four other beach and airborne landing sectors being assaulted by the Americans, British and Canadians on an almost ninety kilometer long front on the Normandy coast.)* The sight was eerie, and it was now clear to us that things were about to get ugly. I knelt in my foxhole and prayed quietly...

Suddenly, we heard the dull drone of aircraft motors coming from the sea. The noise got louder and louder, and the roar of the motors rose to a hellish thunder as a powerful, ghostly fleet of bombers came directly at us in the grey, cloudy sky. Everyone jumped into the bunkers or shelters; I sought cover in my machine gun pit. Then, as quickly as they had come, the broad waves of heavy bombers passed over our heads, and were gone. Immediately thereafter, their load came howling, whistling and crashing down. The bombs fell like heavy rain, and the first hit barely fifty meters behind our strongpoint. Everything started to shake, even our small, dug-in observation post vibrated from the detonations, and earth and chunks of limestone fell around close to us - but the bombers missed their target. *(The objective of the pilots of the 446 B-24 bombers and their 1,285 tons of bombs was the destruction of the 15 German strongpoints. But because of the thick clouds, the bomber formations from England were forced to fly, and to drop their bombs on instruments. In order to avoid placing their own naval fleet in danger, the calculated point for dropping the bombs was shifted several seconds to the rear. Because of this, 13,000 very heavy bombs missed their target - an average of 36 bombs, with a total weight of 3.6 tons, per German soldier in this sector...!)*

The thunder and crashing of the heavy air attack was hardly over when a thundering, hellish barrage from the sea began. Rockets and shells of the heaviest calibers thumped down continuously on our positions. The ground of the entire line of high coastal bluffs trembled under the head-on attack, and the air vibrated. Thick, yellow, choking dust filled the air. The sky was darkened by dense smoke, and clouds of dirt; in between there were the flashes of thundering explosions, and it seemed as though the whole world would sink down in a howling and crashing inferno of bursting shells. On the slope of our position, dry grass and gorse bushes began to burn. However, most of the shells of this barrage also hit too far above the strongpoint, and did little damage. *(I only noticed later that I had sustained a hearing loss from the noise and the pressure of the air from the exploding shells which lasted all my life.)* But this barrage had left me perceptibly more belligerent...

Somewhere along the line I had left my machine gun position during a short lull in the firing, and had gone into the adjacent trench. Then the shells started falling again, and tall fountains of earth rose up all around me. It smelled like the remains of a fire, and the air tasted bitter. A completely frightened Technical Sgt. Fack cowered in the entrance of the observation post bunker; his entire body shivered and trembled. During the bombardment he had lost his pistol. I picked it up and gave it back to him. He looked at me with a face contorted by fear, and flickering eyes.

The strongpoint as seen from the sea. On June 6, 1944, the GI.'s had more than 500 meters of mined and barricaded beach to cross - in the face of our defensive fire... My machine gun position (2) was only seven meters from the observation post bunker (1).

A shell came howling at us and hit in the immediate vicinity of the zig-zag trench *(A trench that changed direction every few meters, to prevent fragments of a shell landing in it from flying around very far)*. I received a sudden, hard blow on the visor of my helmet, and then there was something rolling around on the ground between my legs; it was the size of a small can of milk, and as I went to pick it up it burned me on the finger. The thick, heavy and hot brass ring was a piece of the fuse of the shell. At that moment, Lt. Frerking peered out of the bunker and called to me through the roar:

"Are you all right?"

"Yes!", I shouted back, "I've just had this chunk land on my head!"

I quickly handed him the heavy metal part that was still so hot that he immediately dropped it. Then I called out to him:

"If they keep on shooting like this, something is going to happen here!"

Frerking scolded me because I hadn't sought shelter in the dugout, instead of which I had stayed in the trench. He called out:

"So you still haven't had enough...!"

The lieutenant had worried about me, but he appeared to me suddenly to be noticeably transformed - as if he didn't believe he would survive that which lay before us...

At shortly before 0630, after the heavy salvos of the battleships had stopped, I noticed a large, thin and tall boat in our bay, coming from the northeast toward our wide, ebb-tide beach directly in front of our sector, and 600 meters from Strongpoint WN 62. It was a troop landing ship with a shallow hull and a pointed bow, on either side of which large gangplanks were lowered. A large number of soldiers appeared at the railing, and began to go down the gangplanks, loaded down with weapons and equipment. One could see it clearly. Though we had always spoken of the "Tommies" we expected, I could see immediately from the shape of the helmets and the large, white letters, US, on the bow of the transport that they were Americans. They descended the gangplanks calmly, in orderly columns, and jumped into the cold, chest- to shoulder-high water. Many went under for a moment and, half swimming, half wading, they began to move slowly toward the beach in front of our strongpoint.

At this time it was almost completely quiet in the bay, and not a single shot was being fired. We had strict orders to wait until the G.I.'s were only about 400 meters from the upper beach, and in knee-deep water. I ran to the communications bunker about twenty meters distant, and called:

The first U.S. soldiers leave an LCI,L (Landing Craft Infantry, Large). Located just at the boundary between Easy Red and Fox Green sectors.

"Now it's starting; they're landing!

The operators, who were constantly busy with the telephone and radio, couldn't leave their bunker, and for that reason they couldn't know what was going on outside. One of them said to me:

"Hein, when you can, let us know what is going on down there on the beach ..."

Then I ran back through the trench the few steps to my machine gun.

By that time, more and more soldiers had disembarked from the transport *(an LCI,L carried about 150 soldiers)*. After the Americans got a footing, they waded in two long columns, one behind the other, through the water, and each held on to the belt of the one in front with his left hand. Everything went in such a cool and orderly way, as if it they were merely conducting a training exercise. *(The Americans had clearly thought, after the bombing and the heavy naval barrage, that they could count on a complete absence of resistance from the German side.)*

Lieutenant Frerking appeared next to me in the trench, and we observed how the Americans, loaded down with weapons and equipment, toiled slowly forward, completely defenseless, through the high swells of the cold salt water. It was clear to us that the GI.'s down there were about to enter into their own slaughterhouse.

"Poor swine....", Frerking said softly to himself; then he went down into the bunker to give the coordinates and firing order for the artillery. As I turned back to my machine gun position I also had the feeling that I was ascending a scaffold...

It had lasted about five minutes until the Americans *(units of the 1ˢᵗ U.S. Infantry Division)* reached the shallow water. I noticed then, for the first time that day, that there were soldiers of Grenadier Regiment 726 at our strongpoint for, somewhat further down beneath my machine gun position, a sergeant and another infantryman were trying frantically to get a machine gun *(MG 34)* into action - but it wasn't working.

I'm not the type to look for trouble; I hadn't thought of any such thing: whatever for? Behind me, the entrance to the strongpoint was mined - and barricaded with a thick barrier of barbed wire. *(That the heavy naval bombardment had totally torn up and disarranged everything up there I learned only later.)* Anyway, I was a soldier; a soldier who was going to be attacked, and as such I now had to defend myself. I moved the safety lock of my machine gun to the off position and began to fire. I could see the water spouts where my machine gun bursts were hitting, and when the little fountains got close to the GI.'s, they threw themselves down. After only a few seconds, panic broke out among the Americans. They all lay in the shallow, cold water; many tried to get to the most forward beach obstacles to find some cover behind them. Soon the first corpses drifted about in the waves of the slowly rising tide. I fired further among the many dark forms in the water, which were still about 300 meters from the upper beach. After a little while, all the GI.'s on the beach had been brought down. Suddenly, I had the impression that mine was the only

(photomontage)

My machine gun position was at the end of the trench, and from my position 30 meters above the sea on the sloping coastal hill, I started firing at the G.I.'s from a distance of almost 500 meters. Later, as the tide rose, the distance was little more than 150 meters.

machine gun in our entire sector that had fired. It is true that my machine gun made so much noise that I could hardly have heard the others; nevertheless it seemed to me that I actually had fired completely alone, as I only observed the panicky reaction of the Americans at those places in the water where I had aimed...

I must state here that I had concentrated exclusively on the incoming Americans. I was not even aware of the any hits of our own artillery. My remembered impressions come from my own subjective sense in a psychologically very stressful situation.

Then I noticed that tumultuous scenes were playing out on the deck of the troop transport, and on the gangplanks on either side. It was clear that the G.I.'s who had seen what had just happened to their comrades were refusing to go down and jump into the blood-colored water. But they had to go down - and I began to fire again. Few G.I.'s reached the upper beach...

After there were no more soldiers coming down from the transport, and there were no more to be seen on it, there was a pause. I didn't know what would happen now, and went to the small observation post where Frerking was already standing on the flat roof. I offered him a cigarette, and although he was not a smoker, he took it. Our hands shook as we lit the cigarettes...

Suddenly a whole swarm of landing craft approached the bay. I could see clearly how the small boats crowded with G.I.'s struggled in the heavy seas, and moved forward only slowly. About thirty troops crouched in each boat. The drone of the motors got louder and louder, and echoed in the entire bay.

Something was burning on the water, and it seemed ages until the keel-less boats grounded on the sand of the beach. Just at that moment I noticed that down below, almost up to the upper beach, there was a thin metal staff about three meters high, with a red pennant attached. *(A G.I. of the first wave who must have escaped my notice had, no doubt, put it up as an orientation mark for the following landing craft - red for the sector "Easy Red", in front of WN 62, immediately next to "Fox Green" sector.)* One of the first landing craft headed right for this pennant. I had used the time after firing the first thousand rounds to change out the still-hot barrel of my machine gun for a new one. It was so hot that I got a painful burn on my fingers. Then the wide, steel ramp of the small boat near the signal pennant fell, and the G.I.'s rushed out. I began to fire again...

Landing craft approached the coast. (In the background, the battleship "Arkansas", from which our position was shelled with 14 inch, 15 inch and 16 inch guns of the extreme largest calibers.)

The landing craft now came in wave after wave, always a whole cluster, in an irregular formation. Each time, there had been a recognizable interval, and then the next wave came in. *(I counted six such assault waves before noon.)* As the boats approached, I concentrated on the ramps. Each time one fell, I began to fire. I had observed, in the meantime, that there was firing from the other strongpoints as well, but soon there was no firing or resistance from them. *(From the height of my machine gun position, however, I couldn't determine how many soldiers there were in WN 62 still firing at the attacking Americans by noon. It was not until I started working on this book that I obtained a schedule of all the German telephone messages of June 6ʰ, 1944. Included therein was a message to Grenadier Regiment 726 at 1012 hours of which an extract reads, "WN 62 firing with only one machine gun. Situation there, however, is critical...")*

The incoming boats came up closer and closer to the higher upper beach as the tide rose *(which increased their peril, as the beach obstacles sank slowly under the surface of the water and became invisible to them).* In the meantime, a number of landing craft, some half sunk, drifted in the waves. The G.I.'s tried to take cover behind beach obstacles not yet

61

covered by the tide, or behind the drifting bodies of their dead comrades. Often it was only possible to see their helmets.

After the ramp had been lowered, the G.I.'s tried to move away from the landing craft as quickly as possible. Our machine gun fire was concentrated on it, as we wanted to prevent their dispersion.

After the landing craft had spit out their living cargo, they pulled back. In the interval until the next wave, I shot at anything that moved in the water and on the beach. Some of the time I used my rifle, because I could target individual soldiers and, at the same time, let the machine gun cool.

The individual waves coming at WN 62, consisting of 10 to 15 landing craft of various types, only brought a few hundred troops to the beach each time *(on all of "Omaha" beach each wave totaled 50 to 60 boats).* When these had been laid low by the machine gun, and the survivors polished off with the rifle, there were intervals of varying length. From time to time I met Frerking on the concrete roof of the observation post. A couple of times in between I ran, crouching, to the communications bunker to tell my comrades there about things on the beach. The totally undone Sgt. Fack continued to cower in the trench in front of the observation post, moaning quietly that it was all over. At some point he left...

Shortly after noon another Technical Sgt. came toward me through the trench half caved-in by the shellfire. He was sort of a latin type, slender, with almost black hair, but very pale, for there was dark blood running from two holes in his throat. His throat had been pierced on the left side, which did not, however, seem to affect his spirit, even though his uniform was soaked through with blood. I was just about to kick open the bolt of my rifle with the heel of my boot, because I could no longer do it by hand. As the sergeant saw what I was doing, he said:

"Young fellow, don't make yourself miserable; the rifle is much too hot."

It had not occurred to me until then that I had burned myself when I gripped the cartridge chamber. While I went back to firing the machine gun, the sergeant ran to our communications bunker and got me another rifle.

"They're not using any weapons down there", he said, and deeploaded the rifle. *("deeploaded" means that, in addition to the five cartridges in the clip, a sixth was loaded directly into the chamber.)* During all of this, the sergeant made me aware of two German infantrymen who were sitting in a foxhole quite near me to the east. They kept loading their rifles, which they then poked up over the wall of the trench and, without being able to see any target at all from their cover, simply fired. *(Their bullets must have come down down somewhere in the distance near the battleships, but certainly never on the beach where the enemy lay.)* The sergeant went over to them and bawled them out. Soon thereafter, they had disappeared. I, on the contrary, felt a further growing combativeness ever since the bleeding sergeant had been with me.

In front of our strongpoint, just to the left, and right on the beach, there was a gravel grinding mill that looked like a large metal funnel, and rested on two large concrete blocks. A conveyor belt led from it to the upper beach. *(Masses of palm-sized gravel the thickness of a thumb lay over the whole length of our beach section which, when ground down, were used for construction of the bunkers. The U.S. tanks bogged down on these same gravel banks in the course of the day.)* The sergeant, who had remained with me for almost the entire time, pointed to this gravel mill below us, and said:

"Down there, another one is running down there...!"

The German machine guns often pounded the wooden landing craft even before the ramp was lowered. Then the closely packed GI.'s on the boats tried to take cover between their comrades. Panic often broke out among them. Their position must have been terrible...

Now it occurred to me for the first time how many dead there were down there on the beach, washed up by the rising tide and the high waves. In a roughly three hundred meter-long, and meters-wide ribbon of bloody slime, there were hundreds and hundreds of lifeless bodies of American soldiers - in places piled on top of each other. Wounded moved around in the bloody, watery slime, mostly creeping, trying to get to the upper beach to get some cover behind its embankment about one-and-a-half meters high, and I could still see only fifty to sixty G.I.'s who, one-by-one, would occasionally run around in a crouch.

The G.I.'s tried to take cover behind the beach obstacles and the bodies of their fallen comrades in the face of the awful machine gun fire coming at them from the strongpoints. This was the worst thing they could have done, as it provided the German soldiers an opportunity for targeted fire. For them there was only a single way to escape the deadly danger namely to get off the beach as quickly as possible...

The G.I. the sergeant had pointed out to me was now almost reaching the upper beach, and I could see that he had something on his back that looked like large metal flasks - like fuel tanks of a flame thrower - and a flame thrower burst, with its roughly one thousand degree heat, might be able to reach from the upper beach to my MG foxhole...I took the loaded rifle from the sergeant, aimed, and shot at the G.I.. He tried immediately to take cover behind the large gravel mill. *(If you shot at soldiers with a machine gun, they would hit the ground for cover immediately. Only when, after the burst, just a few were left standing, could you know if, and how many, had been hit. If you shot with a rifle you would know immediately if someone had been hit. In contrast to machine gun traverse fire, where hits were more likely to have been the result of chance, a rifle can be aimed over some distance at the upper body, which presents a target with the greatest probability of a successful hit.)* The G.I. still had no cover, and I loaded and shot again. His helmet flew off his head, tumbled over the sand of the beach, and was immediately washed away in the shallow waves of the receding tide. The G.I. jerked to a stop, sank heavily to his knees; his chin fell to his chest, and then he toppled slowly forward and fell on his face... *(My aim must have been too high, torn through his helmet and got him right in the head.)* At that moment I became really aware for the first time of what I actually had been doing - killing men...

Over time, the sergeant had often disappeared, and then always come back with more machine gun ammunition for me. He had brought me at least 8,000 rounds where from I didn't know. But after something more than an hour, it struck me that he was no longer there. *(He had, at some point, left without a word...)*

Suddenly, while I was again firing the machine gun, there was a bright, loud report directly in front of me. Something flew at me from the muzzle of my machine gun, and it was as though I had been hit in the face with a whip right under my right eye. The burning pain made me reach reflexively for my face - my finger was immediately covered with blood. And as I felt the flesh under my eye swelling, I noticed that the front sight was missing from the barrel of my machine gun. It had been torn off by what was apparently a well aimed shot, and hit me in the face. I was now even more furious, and proceeded to aim my brutal fire at the remaining G.I.'s on the beach in front of WN 62. *(As I later discovered, the American attack was strongest in our sector in front of Colleville. This circumstance arose not only from the fact that the Americans wanted to open this important route inland for their tanks and supplies as quickly as possible - one of six, that was also the least barricaded but also because so many of their landing craft had been carried here by the strong current from the west. Their confusion was increased because many landed in a sector about which they had not been briefed.)*

Fear... In a hail of machine gun fire, a GI. drifts closer to the beach on the rising tide.

Around 1400 I noticed six U.S. tanks on the upper beach somewhat further left of me, moving toward our sector *(from the direction of St. Laurent and "Easy Green" sector). I was unaware of the many amphibious tanks that had already been sunk on their way to the beach in the heavy seas, and in which countless tragedies had played out. I had concentrated solely on the beach in front of my strongpoint, and enough happened there. Also, the landing craft that come ashore in the neighboring sectors moved only on the edge of my field of vision - and zone of fire.*

Meanwhile, I had shot many thousands of rounds from my machine gun and now had to switch to ammunition made for night fighting. *(Every fifth bullet in these ammunition belts was a tracer bullet.)* Although I was aware of the risk that the Americans would be more able to identify my exact position when I fired, I began to shoot. *(I could no lon-ger use the rifle, as my right eye had, meanwhile, become completely swollen shut by the effects of the flying gun sight.)*

This landing craft approached our sector towards 1,100. In the back-ground, to the right, the valley in front of Colleville can be seen. About halfway up the rising slope on the right (not in the photo) was WN 62. On the beach in front of the small WN 61 are destroyed U.S. tanks and half-sunken landing craft.

Shortly thereafter, a shell landed directly in front of my position; a dark fountain of dirt and sandstone tore my machine gun right out of my hands while I was firing, and tossed it back over me. Whereupon, I hauled the machine gun back and examined it for a moment for possible damage, but couldn't see any. Then I concentrated again on the Ameri-cans below on the beach. Additional landing craft had approached, and I pounded away again among the G.I.'s running out of them. A moment later my machine gun was again torn away by a shell that landed close by me, and within ten minutes twice more. *(I thought that one of the six tanks that had landed on the beach in the meantime had fired on my small machine gun position. I learned only later that it had been the U.S. De-*

stroyer "Frankford" that had targeted me with a number of rounds, from a distance of about three kilometers - my conspicuous tracer ammunition had given away my position.)

Meanwhile, there were increasing troop movements on the upper beach. More and more Americans had landed in all of "Omaha" bay, and a number of U.S. tanks had also been able to reach land. I had not been able to observe from my position that, starting as early as 0800, small groups of G.I.'s had moved up the heights only several hundred meters away on either side of our strongpoint, and advanced to our rear - and larger numbers after 1000 hours.

From my position I couldn't know the full extent of the individual trage-dies that played out in front of our sector. Here, medics of the 5th U.S. Engineer Brigade that landed in front of our strongpoint give a transfusion to a severely wounded soldier on the beach in front of the Colleville valley.

It had been clear to me for some time that we would have to give up our position in the foreseeable future and retreat, as our ammunition would inevitably run out at some point. It had been a long time since I had seen any soldiers of the 716th Grenadier Regiment. But for the time being

I kept on shooting, for the risk of being hit by a shell or a bullet during a withdrawal up the sloping height seemed to me to be not insignificant. Strangely, I was not worried about being hit in my foxhole. Besides which, I thought the entrance to WN 62 at the top of the rise was still firmly barricaded.

From 1500 on, I saw many more Americans only some 250 meters to the west, climbing the sloping heights in long columns. *(Since about 1200 I had been able to see many U.S. Soldiers in dark columns climbing the slopes between St. Laurent and Vierville, almost five kilometers distant from my position.)* Just then, I noticed that our observation post bunker had been taken under fire. One round had hit the concrete of the upper edge of the one-and-a-half meter wide observation aperture and made a crackling explosion. I ran quickly to the bunker to see what had happened to the two inside; Lt. Grass came limping out, supported by Lt. Frerking. When he saw my troubled and questioning look he explained:

"It caught me on the knee..."

Only a small, three-cornered rip in his riding britches revealed that a small shell fragment had hit him in the kneecap. As they crept slowly up the half-buried trench to the communications bunker, Frerking said to me:

"It's now time for all of us to get out and abandon our position up here..."

The barrel of my machine gun had, meanwhile, lost its rifling some time earlier, and had become so hot that dry grass caught fire on its muzzle. I had fired more than 12,000 rounds from the weapon. The two rifles, with which I had shot roughly 400 rounds, were also completely overheated. I knew the time had come when all was lost. Although I took the machine gun with me, loaded with a fifty-cartridge drum, I didn't want to kill anyone else - it was enough...

More and more Americans appeared to our side. I ran the several meters to the communications bunker. Now I saw for the first time that the entire slope of our strongpoint had been completely dug up by the shellfire of the naval artillery. I barked at the radio operators, Herbert Schulz and Kurt Wernecke, that we were now going to withdraw.

As we three traversed the totally devastated trench, Lt. Frerking, Lt. Grass and Sgt. Beermann were already waiting for us. Their helmets and uniforms were covered with light colored dust. Lt. Frerking had hung a long machine gun belt with about a hundred cartridges around his neck

- although I was the only one who still had a machine gun. The communication trench was less than half its original depth on account of the dirt flung around by the barrage. A distraught soldier of the 726th crouched with us artillerymen. He was the only German infantryman I had seen in hours. Lt. Frerking said to him:

"You jump out first and start out carefully to the rear. I'll jump out next, then Pfc. Severloh will follow me, and then the others..."

The infantryman jumped immediately from the trench, ran crouching, diagonally to the left, and tried to take cover behind the nearby excavation spoil of a yet-to-be-built bunker. A regular hailstorm of bullets rained down on the mound immediately. The Americans had, by this time, moved up to the western side of the strongpoint. Down below they had finally succeeded in crossing the upper beach and reaching the foot of the coastal slope. G.I.'s lay all over down there under good cover, and had concentrated their fire on us *(since, by this time, we were the last German soldiers in this sector).*

The observation embrasure of the observation post hit by a shell.

After the first of us had withdrawn, the Americans obviously were more alert, and it was clear that they would shoot at us. It was clear that, whatever we did, it had to be done quickly if we wanted to get out alive.

Then Frerking turned to me. He looked at me solemnly, quickly eyed

71

my painful, swollen face.

"You go next, Hein - take care...", he said, contradicting his earlier order, and held his hand out to me. He had addressed me with the familiar "du" for the first time. We didn't have time to say much more. These last seconds of our parting were full of sad misgivings. Silently, we shook hands - only a short, much too short, bizarre moment. A feeling of sympathy, warmth, and attachment welled up again quickly in me and, simultaneously, a deep melancholy. Why this unusual farewell, so often reserved for final leave-takings? Then I clutched my machine gun and jumped from the shallow trench.

Just as I left the trench *(it was just at 1530 hours)*, it crossed my mind that I shouldn't run to the left, as the G.I.'s certainly had the mound of earth clearly in their sights. So I ran somewhat to the right, and was lucky enough, after only a few meters, to find a deep shell hole into which I could jump. A couple of rifle bullets whipped near me into the sand, and then I jumped into the next hole. The American bullets greeted me again.

The last soldiers remaining at WN 62 had gathered in the middle of the communication trench between the observation post (right foreground) and the communications bunker (middle above).

The heavy aerial bombardment at dawn, and the subsequent barrage of the naval artillery had created many deep, almost adjacent bomb craters and shell holes above on the plateau. I was able, crouching at times,

72

The Americans found many dead German soldiers in the captured German strongpoints of the U.S. "Omaha" landing sector.

to run from one to the next without having to show myself above the normal level of the ground. In this way, the bombs that were supposed to have destroyed me, now had helped me find my way quickly and safely over the hundred meter-plus route out of the zone of immediate danger, up to the terrain behind the highest point of the plateau.

About four hundred meters further behind, I stopped under good cover on a narrow lane that led from St. Laurent to WN 62 (*the present-day road to the U.S. Military Cemetery*). Since I couldn't see any more Americans, I waited for my comrades. It was not long before Kurt Wernecke appeared between the craters. I let him know I was there, and in a moment he was next to me. He was agitated, and told me, breath-lessly, that the others were all dead, and that somehow he had survived. Lieutenant Frerking had been killed by a shot to his head. I was very badly shaken, as no news that could have reached me at that moment could have been worse...

Wernecke and I then set off in an easterly direction. I still had my machine gun with me; he had no weapon. Shortly thereafter, we came to the anti-tank gun that was still positioned on the reverse slope of WN 62, where its weapon had been trained on the lower lying road leading from the beach to Colleville. *(In the next few minutes, as I learned later, they took out a Sherman tank that was attempting to advance on the village.)*

Twenty year-old Kurt Wernecke was a Pfc. radio operator of our battery,stationed at WN 62.

Since, for safety's sake we didn't want to use any path or road, we slid on the seat of our pants down the steep slope to the valley in which lay the road to the strongpoint. We crossed it, ran through the farm across the way, and got to the stables. As we came closer, the sheep in the stables began suddenly to voice loud and panic-stricken bleats. We were badly frightened and ran on further. Then we climbed the slope on the other side to a narrow path halfway up, that led from the sea to Colleville.

Kurt Wernecke and I slid down on the seat of our pants from exactly this spot in the valley directly behind WN 62, ran across the farmstead, and climbed halfway up the opposite slope (left).

Our exhaustion slowly became noticeable. The machine gun I was dragging along with me without a carrying strap became heavy for me. Having got up the hill, worn out, we plodded along further. Suddenly, from somewhere to the right, a machine gun clattered on the other side of the narrow valley we had just crossed. Wernecke spun around in an instant, cried out and shied off to the side a couple of meters as if pushed. It tore his feet out from under him. It hit me at the same time, as I had been walking next to him several meters to the side, and threw me down as well. A burning pain ate at my right hip. The sudden thought that it was, indeed, now all over frightened me. I quickly loosened my suspenders, pulled out my shirt, and examined my wound. Wernecke did the same. He had been hit twice by closely spaced bullets on both his buttocks, and blood was already oozing out, and he was bleeding between his thighs.

I had two equally spaced, finger-sized wounds close to each other, out of which dark blood started immediately to pour, and the hip was quickly swollen. All the same, I had the impression that there was no bullet in my flesh. Despite the burning pain, I could move my right leg. I had fallen on my machine gun, and that had hurt me even further. After I had somewhat examined my wound, I threw my machine gun angrily into the close-by bramble thicket on the hill on which we both lay. I asked Wernecke if he was in shape to go further. He nodded, sighing. *(We were under such unusual psychological pressure that, looking back, we weren't able, really, to feel our pain.)*

We pulled our trousers back up, got painfully to our feet, and hurried to take cover under a stand of trees nearby. There we met the first German infantry of our division; there were ten soldiers of the 916th Regiment. There was a medic with them, who attended immediately to the heavily bleeding Wernecke, and determined that it was only a matter of two shots that had passed clean through him *(and then had also hit me)*.

We were now not far from Strongpoint WN 63 *(which was merely a small, half-buried bunker with no weaponry, and which served only as the command post for Grenadier Regiment 915 and the 3rd Company of Grenadier Regiment 726)*. I told Wernecke that I would go to the bunker to inform the battalion commander, Major Dr. Lohmann, who was stationed there, that there was no one left at WN 62 - except for the dead... Then I left. *(I never saw Kurt Wernecke again and never learned what later became of him.)*

At about 1630, I arrived at the concealed WN 63. *(WN 63 was just at the edge of Colleville and on the narrow road that led to the beach. From outside one could see only an iron door, but inside the bunker there were three small rooms, one behind the other. In the preceding months, when I had driven my battery commander to the observation post at WN 62, we had always stopped here a few minutes so that Frerking and Dr. Lohmann could have a short conversation.)* Now I entered the narrow bunker. There were about twenty-five troops inside, including several severely wounded. Per my orders, I made my report to Major Dr. Lohmann, who looked at me compassionately. I reported emotionally that 1st Lt. Frerking had been killed, according to what I had been told by Wernecke.

I could feel Dr. Lohmann's stress and nervousness, but in spite of it he was very friendly toward me, and said:

"You were Frerking's orderly, weren't you?"

I nodded.

"Lie down for a while over there on the plank bed on the wall", he continued. He had certainly noticed not only my distraction and my wound, but also my utter exhaustion. Then he brought over a medic, who made a close examination of the wounds to my face and my hip, determined that there were no bullets in the wounds, and then administered first aid. *(The two bullets that had gone through Wernecke's buttocks must have been slowed down enough that they could no longer penetrate my hip very deeply. In addition, it occurred to me now that, even more luckily, I had been carrying my thick wallet in my jacket where the bullet hit, and it had dampened the impact.)* Finally, the medic gave me another shot, and spent as I was, I went quickly to sleep.

When Dr. Lohmann awakened me, I had lain for over an hour on the narrow plank bed. It was obvious that more wounded soldiers had come in during that time. Lohmann asked me:

"Are you up to guarding a couple of American prisoners?"

"Yes", I answered, "where are they?"

He motioned with his thumb over his shoulder:

"Outside..."

When I then went outside with a new rifle Dr. Lohmann had given me, there were three Americans standing by the entrance - soldiers of the 1st U.S. Division *(the "Big Red One")*, L Company, 2nd Battalion, 16th Infantry Regiment. They were young fellows exactly like me, who still wore their helmets, and didn't seem to be belligerent. They looked anxiously at me and my rifle. I gave them a sign to sit down on a small stone bench in a recess next to the entrance to the bunker. I sat down next to them.

Rounds were falling in the distance, and soon even nearer to us. It became obvious to me that the front line was no longer on the beach, but had already advanced inland *(still near the coast)*. For some time, the weather had improved from that of the morning, albeit still with a grey, overcast sky, but much lighter. It had by then, become 1800 hours.

The Americans talked softly among themselves, and since I didn't speak English, I didn't understand anything they said. Suddenly one of them spoke to me in perfect Uelzen plattdeutsch *(the "low" German dialect of my hometown):*

"When are you going to shoot?"

I was taken aback, and looked at him dumbfounded. He repeated his question, and I answered:

77

"Have you heard, then, that we generally shoot prisoners?.."

(By this time, the Americans west of us were less than one hundred meters distant.)

The G.I. then asked what would become of them, since they had been told in the U.S.A. that if they were taken prisoner by the Germans, they would be shot at once. Then I realized, finally, that he had not meant to ask by his question when I would shoot my rifle, but when I would execute the three of them. I explained that I couldn't do anything to them as long as they didn't attack me or try to escape, and I saw that he believed me. He also translated our conversation to his comrades. They seemed noticeably relieved.

Then I asked him how it was that he had come to speak the dialect of my hometown. The American then explained to me that his parents had grown up as neighbors in a small village in the vicinity of Uelzen *(about fifty kilometers from my hometown)*. His grandfather had not wanted his son, the heir to a large farm, to marry a servant girl. So the two young people ran away from home and took the train to Hamburg, then a ship to New York, where then they were married.

When I expressed my amazement at his flawless "plattdeutsch", he said:

"This is the way we always spoke at home."

Then the G.I. wanted to know what would happen to him as a prisoner of war. I explained to him that he would doubtless be sent to work for some farmer in the country for some time. He beamed, and said:

"Then I will be in the country my parents came from!"

But unfortunately he didn't know the name of the place from which his parents had come.

Then two dashing-looking German lieutenants suddenly appeared, and brought another American prisoner, who sat down with the others on the stone bench next to the door. On the back of his uniform jacket three large letters were painted: TEX, which indicated that he came from Texas. When he had sat down with us, I pulled the remains of a pack of cigarettes from my jacket; there were three cigarettes. Since, however, there were only five of us, I broke them all in two, handed one piece to each of the Americans, put one between my lips, and kept one-half a cigarette. As I lit the cigarettes for the Americans, I noticed that the Texan had a small, blood-bordered hole on his chest. When he saw that I had noticed it, he turned around and showed me that there was another hole at the same height on his back. He had received a shot clean through him during his landing in front of WN 62 *(probably from me)*, which must have gone through his lung, but he thanked me for the half cigarette and smoked it.

By then, it was almost midnight, and I had been talking with the four U.S. soldiers in my local dialect for the whole time. A four-wheeled cart with two horses had been standing in the nearby meadow for some time. Now - under cover of darkness, in which there was still constant shooting, but finally no longer any American fighter-bombers flying - a few severely wounded were taken from the bunker of WN 63 and loaded on the wagon. The soldier who, the previous night, had secured the entrance to WN 62 after our arrival was also there. Then the cart moved slowly off.

Major Lohmann came and explained that we would all now withdraw to the rear. The cart led the way, followed by three troops of a heavy machine gun unit, one carrying the metal stand, another carried the machine gun, and the third the ammunition. We were a total of 22 German soldiers and four prisoners who now set off on the retreat. Dr. Lohmann came to me and asked which road we should take to reach our 1st Battery at Houtteville. I described the route in general terms.

For safety's sake we avoided the middle of the road, rather kept close to the houses. Nevertheless, hardly fifty meters along, at the churchyard of Colleville, shots rang out through the night close by us. In the dark window openings of the town hall I saw a lot of muzzle blasts. It was clear to us right away that there must be Americans there, and we had noticed for some time that they had come very near; they had already circled around us...

Up until then the four prisoners had been walking behind me. Now, when the shooting started we all hit the ground, seeking cover near the wall of the house. For a moment it seemed as though there were echoing shots coming from every direction in the open square; then it was suddenly as silent as when it had begun. We all rose carefully to continue our march. When I looked around me, my four prisoners were behind me again in the dark. They hadn't taken the proffered opportunity to run back to their comrades under cover of the night. It would also have been an easy thing for them simply to stay where they were...

We now hurried to move out, and turned right not far beyond Colleville, into one of the many narrow sunken roads of Normandy that are flanked by high, ivy-covered stone walls and old trees. But we had hardly entered the dark lane when we encountered a burst of heavy machine gun tracer fire from a distance of about fifty meters. We ducked for cover immediately.

The Colleville town hall today - in 1944, both town hall and school together.

Major Dr. Lohmann and the heavy machine gun squad flung themselves to the left bank of the road, I and the other soldiers, and the prisoners, to the right side. The cart with the severely wounded turned off through a gate into a bordering field at the same time, suddenly picking up speed. The horses had been spooked by the sudden machine gun fire and the sizzling tracer bullets, and had run through, neighing loudly. The cart rumbled off and disappeared into the darkness. A couple of more bursts, and it was quiet again. We waited a moment, and then ran, crouching, to the other side of the lane, the four Americans following me. Major Dr. Lohmann and the machine gun squad were nowhere to be seen...

On the other side, we all ducked down next to the bank. The medic who had taken care of me several hours earlier cowered next to me. He said softly:

"I have to go look after the wounded who are in the cart..."

I tried to dissuade him, but he wanted to follow the cart at all costs. He was *(contrary to military law)* carrying a pistol, a [Luger] P08. Then he disappeared into the darkness. The rest of us stayed quietly where we were, wanting to wait to see how the situation would develop. But after a few minutes we noticed that the medic was back with us. He said, under his breath:

"Here, take this fellow from me..."

In one hand he held his 08, and with the other he was holding by the belt an American whom he had, meanwhile, taken prisoner. The G.I. didn't have a rifle, but we took away his bayonet, hand grenades and ammunition. Then he crouched next to the bank with the other four prisoners, and some time passed in which nothing further happened.

There was another Pfc. in our small party who appeared suddenly at my side and asked me:

"Tell me, can you go on?"

"Yes", I whispered.

"Don't we want to get out of here?"

"Sure", I said, and we considered how we could move out to the east unnoticed, but suddenly someone next to us said:

"If you two try to take off I will shoot you in the ass."

In the slowly breaking dawn we discovered there was a sergeant of the 726th Grenadier Regiment with us. We thought better of it, for he really was right, that if we were spotted, the Americans could have shot all of us. Besides which, we didn't know what had happened to Major Dr. Lohmann and his people after they had disappeared, and why they had disappeared without telling us, and why they had not taken us with them... We had finally, to admit to ourselves that the war was already over for us, and that we were now only a small, lost lot with few weapons and equally few prospects, surrounded by a superior enemy force, and lying somewhere at the end of the earth in a damp, sunken lane.

The sergeant came up right next to me and I felt his agitation; he whispered:

"Tell the Americans we want to surrender..."

Since none of us spoke English, I turned to the prisoner who spoke my own dialect so beautifully and told him that he should call out to his comrades over there in the breaking dawn that we wanted to surrender. He clapped me gently on the shoulder, as if we had been old friends, and then he called out:

"American! American, don't shoot!" Then he described the situation that he and another three Americans had been brought this far by a small group of Germans...

The G.I.'s ahead of us in the lane then wanted to know how many we were. After counting up, we told them we were 18 troops and five prisoners. More than half of us were wounded. When the Americans heard that, they called to us to put all our weapons and ammunition down on the edge of the road, and come up over the bank and through the thicket with our hands up.

Right up until that moment I had translated our curious conversation via the Uelzen "plattdeutsch", but now I experienced a sense of deep resignation; the whole struggle, all the sacrifice, the enormous exertion of physical and psychological effort, the fear, the pain and the terrible killing - was it all suddenly to have been for naught? I thought also of Frerking, and felt the warm tears welling up in my eyes and rolling down my swollen face. Now it was over...

Prisoner of War

Now, one after the other, we climbed the embankment of the sunken road and pushed through the thick underbrush. On the meadow behind, in the growing daylight, stood a group of almost thirty Americans, their rifles and automatic weapons at the ready, aimed directly at us. I went last, with the five G.I.'s who had, until just now, been our prisoners, and still had my rifle with me. The American next to me said:

"Now don't shoot, don't shoot!"

I told him I thought his comrades over there were about to pull the trigger and that we would all be killed, but then he explained quickly:

They're not going to shoot…!"

The Americans approached us slowly, their weapons still aimed at us. The G.I. to my side who, in that instant, was again free, laid his hand on my shoulder and continued in the familiar dialect:

"But now you have to go…"

I took the bolt out of my rifle and threw it away, surrendered the weapon to him, and followed the others on the large meadow. It had just become 0400 hours, and dawn was breaking.

The Americans who had taken us prisoner belonged to the 2nd Battalion, 16th Infantry Regiment of the 1st Division *("Big Red One")*

The 16th Infantry Regiment of "The Big Red One" was composed of soldiers, most of whom came from New York and were, on that account, given the nickname "Subway Soldiers" in the U.S. Army. They were the elite of the American army, but since their landing craft had been forced

82

by the current far from their assigned landing zone (only two landing craft reached their assigned location), they had mostly to come ashore in front of my sector - or had tried to. They were, then, precisely those soldiers on whom I had fired so industriously... (I learned later that in one of the landing craft only 7 out of 32 troops - though wounded - had reached the upper beach alive...)

Not far away stood the cart pulled into the large meadow by the horses during the night. The untreated, severely wounded were still lying on the cart; one of the horses lay dead in the harness. The Americans now ordered us to lay down our belts, to empty our pockets, and to hand over everything: all our personal effects, even wallets and pay books. I still had two hand grenades on me, put them down quickly on the grass and covered the two of them with handkerchiefs that I also had on me. Then we all had to line up, raise our hands, and turn around. The Americans still had their weapons at the ready, spoke quietly among themselves, and I thought the last moment of my life had now arrived...

A moment later we were permitted to turn around and pick up our personal belongings. An American officer came over and said, in fluent high-class German:

"You may put your belts back on, and also your side arms *(bayonets)*. But I will tell you that we would have had good grounds to shoot you, on account of the losses you inflicted on us..."

I hoped, silently, that there were no longer any witnesses to my yesterday's actions...

By then, it had become daylight, and we were informed that we were to hike back to Vierville. We were to put the severely wounded from the cart on stretchers and take them with us. With a comrade, I carried the soldier who had secured the entrance to WN 62 after Lt. Frerking and I had arrived the night before. We moved out, guarded by a dozen Americans.

During our march, the U.S. officer had a conversation with one of our people near me. I heard him explain that he had been born in Germany, had served as a sergeant in the pre-war army, and had fallen in love one day with a girl who was also the object of the attentions of another, also a sergeant. The two had dueled *(which had been forbidden for a long time)*, and he had killed his rival. Whereupon he had fled to Switzerland, and from there to the U.S.A.. He had enlisted there in the army years earlier. On the day before, on June 6th, he had been landed on *Omaha*.

After a while we were allowed a break. My comrade and I put down the wounded soldier on the stretcher. In doing that, the sleeve of my jacket pulled up to reveal my wristwatch, which hung somewhat loose on my wrist. A Ranger who had accompanied us as a guard saw my watch, came over to me, took my wrist, opened the catch and silently took my watch off. He was an unattractive, tough looking type with a fearsome, Iroquois haircut *(where only a brush of hair three fingers-wide remained, after all the hair on the sides had been shaved),* and I could see conspicuous prison numbers tattooed on the left side of his skull. *(The Americans had deployed many hardened criminals right in the front elements of attacking troops.)* Then he left with my watch.

The strenuous and long march to the prisoner assembly area at Vierville with the severely wounded. On the stretcher, which three other comrades and I (middle of photo) had to carry more than six kilometers, lay a soldier with a leg wound who had met Lt. Frerking and me at the entrance to WN 62 on the night of June 6th.

It was less the loss of my wristwatch that outraged me, rather much more the fact that a delicate silver chain with a pendant in the form of a painted, green cloverleaf had hung on it. *(Lisa had given it to me during*

our time in Brunswick, on the day before I was to leave for France.) Since
the silver chain was too small for my wrist, I had wound it decoratively
around my watch and the band. I didn't want to leave it to this criminal,
ran over behind him, grabbed his wrist and tore off the little chain with
the cloverleaf. The Ranger cursed, unslung his rifle and reacted very
menacingly. Two of his comrades quickly interceded and prevented him
from coming after me.

When finally, towards noon, after the six kilometer-long march, we
arrived tired and spent at the devastated promenade in front of Vierville,
the Americans had already set up a large compound. It swarmed with
soldiers. Even as we were on the march we encountered large numbers of
G.I.'s, and columns of trucks and tanks, and the fighter-bombers howled
overhead. The large casemate at Strongpoint WN 72 in which the 8.8 cm.
cannon is *(even today)* located, now served the Americans as a command
post. On the devastated beach, between countless wrecks of landing
craft, there were almost a hundred ships of all sizes, and masses of soldiers and vehicles were constantly being offloaded. Over the warships
that had, in the meantime, come in closer to the shore, glistened the silver
grey, zeppelin-like barrage balloons that served as antiaircraft defense
- but they might have been dispensed with completely, as I never saw a
single plane of the German Luftwaffe *(Air Force)*...

A large medical tent had been set up in the American compound.
There we finally set down the stretchers carrying our severely wounded
comrades. A U.S. medic who had noticed my face and hip wounds came
over to me and wanted to treat me as well, but I declined brusquely;
I already had a snoot full of the Americans and didn't want to let them lay
another hand on me.

Then we had to climb the high, steep bluff to the plateau that lay west
of the valley in front of Vierville. Above, on a grassy area, the Americans
had set up a large, temporary prisoner-of-war camp. From up there we
had a good view of the completely ravaged *(Omaha)* beach. Masses of
wrecks of landing craft drifted around all up and down the beach. On the
beach and the upper beach there were destroyed tanks, and some of the
wrecked vehicles still smoldered from time to time. I could see troops
who were clearing off the beach, with the help of bulldozers and power
shovels. Huge numbers of American troops, as well as immense quantities of war materiel were offloaded to the beach without interruption.
The beach resembled a gigantic, swarming anthill.

Captured German soldiers in American captivity on the day after D-Day.

We lay down, exhausted, on the meadow, but despite our fatigue hardly anyone could sleep; our hunger and thirst were too great. *(I had buttered my last slice of bread up in WN 62 during the night of June 6ᵗʰ and eaten it shortly before the bombardment had begun. For most of my comrades it was no different.)* Before we were finally fed, however, the Americans set up cameras and movie cameras *(which took a long time),* to document the provisioning of poor, mistreated German prisoners of war for posterity...

By this time it was nearly 1900 hours, and during the afternoon occasional other German prisoners were brought in. Now Capt. Wilkening arrived, with two other soldiers of the 3ʳᵈ Battery. We learned from him that the German infantry had been reinforced and come closer. The hope stirred in us that we would be freed. Nonetheless, our feelings were ambivalent, as we really didn't want any more fighting...

I couldn't resist a certain satisfaction in knowing that Wilkening had also been captured. He had always remained the same person he had been earlier in Russia. When he heard us complain of hunger, he said, grinning cynically, that we should all kindly lie down on the meadow and eat grass like all cattle...After a long wait, however, a U.S. soldier finally called out in perfect German:

"Rations have arrived!"

View of disembarking American supply troops, from the heights at Vierville at the western flank of "Omaha Beach".

During the course of the next day, June 8th, two G.I.'s brought my familiar comrade, Adolf Schiller, to the prisoner of war camp at Vierville. He looked terrible, and his uniform was streaked with blood; he had been wounded in the face and mouth, and his shoulder and arm. Schiller and the young comrade with him had been situated at WN 61, on the other side of the Colleville valley and about 900 meters from WN 62 as the crow flies. Both of them had been assigned to the observation post of the 3rd Battery of our Artillery Regiment 352.

Adolf explained to me that the Americans had been unable to take his strongpoint in the course of the 6th of June, but had surrounded and besieged it until the evening of the 7th, and not until darkness had he been able to escape. He had then hidden during the night of June 7-8 in a deserted Sherman tank. The tank had bogged down in the gravel bank in front of WN 62 *(in "Easy Red" sector)* after the landing, and later had been abandoned by its crew. On the next day, after he had left the tank, he was taken prisoner by two G.I.'s. One of the Americans had then suggested that, in view of the many dead G.I.'s on the beach, it would be better to shoot him on the spot rather than taking him to the prisoner of war camp. Adolf Schiller reacted to that in a panic, ran to the sea, threw himself into the water and wanted to swim to safety. He reported further that the Americans had first called out to him, then had aimed and shot at him. Two bullets went through his left shoulder, one hit his cheek; then he had given up his attempted flight.

While Adolf Schiller was still telling me this story, two American medics appeared, who gave us to understand that we *(Adolf and I)* should go to their medical tent, as they wanted to treat us. When, however, we refused to follow them, they grabbed us by the arm to tug us along with them. We hit them on their hands. We still didn't want to be treated by Americans - we were still too frustrated...

Then Adolf told me about what he had seen from his observation post at WN 61, and that he had been able to observe quite clearly what havoc my machine gun fire had actually wreaked down there on the beach. *(To explain, let me mention that there is at the forward end of the upper beach - even today - an almost vertical bank, up to one-and-a-half meters high in places, that falls almost vertically to the beach. It stretches over a length of about 450 meters. The soldiers who had landed tried, on the one hand, to take cover behind this embankment, while, at the same time, it hid from my view the masses of dead Americans that drifted slowly up on the rising tide during the course of the morning.)* When, then, on June 8th Adolf Schiller and the young soldier were led all the way down the beach to Vierville by the Americans as prisoners, the two could see the full terrible effect of the hail of bullets the G.I.'s had received from WN 62.

Meanwhile, repeated high tides had come in, and had washed ashore heaps of corpses in front of the steep embankment over a length of more than 300 meters. The two comrades reported what they had seen, visibly taken aback and upset. *(Adolf Schiller's unrealistic estimate, that the dead were heaped three meters high, reflects the frightful impression that he had taken away from this experience in his memory...)*

By June 8^{th,} our hopes of being freed had evaporated, and the next day we had to fall in and walk in columns down to the beach. There we boarded a number of landing craft and were taken to a troop transport that lay further out. On the beach, before boarding, the officers and non-commissioned officers were separated from the troops *(as a precaution against possible reprisals by the soldiers against their superiors)*.

On June 10th, we arrived at Portland *(peninsula on the British channel coast)*. There we had to take off all our clothes and, despite cool weather, we had to spend the whole day naked with our clothes in our arms. Perhaps the Americans were afraid of us, perhaps it was only an utterly mean and humiliating form of harassment. Then, every tenth one of us, chosen at random, was searched for lice. They cut several broad hanks from our hair; but we didn't have any lice at all. When we were finally allowed to put our trousers back on, they blew thick clouds of white poison powder into them from a large spray gun *(to kill the lice of which we had absolutely none)*. The next morning we were transported by train to Glasgow, in southern Scotland.

Since my account is intended to be limited to my experiences on *Omaha Beach*, I will limit the various locations of my captivity as a prisoner of war to the dates *(with the exception of two of these subsequent episodes)*:

06/17/1944	On the "Queen Mary" to the USA
06/24/1944	Disembark in Boston
06/27/1944	By train to the state of Mississippi; to POW camp McCain.
07/15/1944	Transfer to Memphis, Tennessee
08/05/1944	Back to McCain
08/08/1944	To cotton harvest at Clarksdale
02/16/1945	Transfer to Camp Blanding, Florida
02/25/1945	To Homestead for potato harvest
03/09/1945	To Hastings
04/15/1945	To Bel Haven, Miami, Florida, for work in Miami Beach hotel
02/16/1946	Transfer to Camp Candle for potato harvest
03/02/1946	Transfer to Camp Forrest, Tennessee
03/06/1946	To discharge camp, Camp Shanks, New York
03/22/1946	Depart the USA on board the "Wheaton Victory"
03/31/1946	Arrive in Antwerp, Belgium and in POW Camp 2218U at Velvorde

04/05/1946	Transfer to Camp 2221D at Velvorde
05/25/1946	Transfer to Camp 2225 at Antwerp
05/26/1946	On board the "Aahus" to England
05/27/1946	Land at Tilbury
05/28/1946	Departure to Scotland, Gosfort Camp at Longniddry
06/24/1946	28 days in the stockade *(for unauthorized possession of foodstuffs)*
07/16/1946	Transfer to Camp 278 at Clapham-Badford, Hostel 4
01/20/1947	Transfer to Corronation
04/02/1947	Transfer to Hostel 1 at Clapham-Badford

In the course of my captivity there were a lot of experiences and observations that would be quite worth reporting; like the Fall day of 1944 in the POW camp at Clarksdale, Mississippi, when we were promised that we would have the rest of the day off if we completed the harvest of the modest balance of a cotton field:

Under the usual surveillance of two or three guards *(soldiers)* - with shotguns*(!)* we 50 men began to harvest the cotton, stuff it in sacks, drag them to the trucks and empty them. Sweat rolled off our bodies in streams, but we were finished with the strenuous work shortly after noon. But instead of the promised afternoon off, we weren't taken back to the camp, but rather to the next cotton field - to harvest it. When we grumbled about it, we were promised again that we should have the rest of the day off if we hurried. We pulled ourselves together again and went at the work. By now we already had a certain routine, but before we finished with the huge field it began to grow dark. After we had loaded the last large, bulging sack of cotton on one of the trucks, we were ordered to harvest yet a third field - piece by piece. We 50 prisoners of war stood as *one* man, arms folded - no! Now we were accused of mutiny - even though it had become dark by this time...

A detail of additional soldiers was called in, and soon thereafter, almost twenty soldiers arrived. A number of cotton trucks were driven in around us in a large circle. We stood there in the bright light of the headlights, and a major ordered us to continue the work, but we continued to refuse firmly. Then the order was given to the soldiers to aim their weapons at us. My comrade, Helmut Krowatz, raised his shirt, pointed to his heart, and shouted to the soldiers:

"Shoot here!"

There was a moment of silence, then the major ordered a soldier who

was standing near Krowatz:
"Shoot this man!"
But there was no shot...
We could all see clearly that the whole spectacle of the soldiers and their aimed weapons, and the order to shoot, were sheer psychoterror - nothing else...
Then the major commanded us to at least go into the third field that lay immediately next to us. But when he saw that we continued to refuse this order as well, ordered that we all should take a single step into the field, or at least put one foot in, and then everything would be all right and it would all be over. But not one of us moved as much as a single centimeter from where we were standing

A moment later, we were loaded into the military trucks and were finally taken back to the camp - and as punishment confined for 21 days in several large, specially fenced-in tents. But instead of the 21 days to which we had been sentenced, they released us after only 10 days to be sent back immediately to the cotton fields...

But something else that happened in the USA, and which had a much more tragic background, seems to me to be of more importance than a spiteful abuse of our labor. This had happened to me only a few days after my arrival at Camp McCain at the beginning of my captivity in the USA, and engraved itself deeply in my consciousness:

A comrade sitting next to me in front of our tent leafed through an already somewhat tattered copy of the American magazine, *Star*. It was the first edition to have appeared after *D-Day* and was only a week or two old; it contained many reports and photographs of *D-Day*. At that time I didn't yet have a command of the English language, so I looked rather lackadaisically at the pages my comrade turned. But at the last moment, as he threw the magazine to the ground with the words, "Shitty War", a striking picture caught my attention - a picture of the old church tower of Colleville that was so familiar to me. I picked up the *Star* again, looked for the page - and there it was, my old church tower, but almost completely destroyed by shellfire. I asked my comrade to read me the article and translate it. I thought right away of my former battery commander, Bernhard Frerking and whether there might be something to found here about him and his death. No word about it, but instead, information that moved me deeply and confirmed the horror and the extent of the part I had played in the events in front of WN 62 - about which Adolf Schiller had already told me in the POW camp on the plateau at Vierville. In the magazine the events on *Omaha Beach* in U.S. sector *Easy Red* were described *(I remember clearly the first words of English I knew):*

"Weapons-carrying men could not, in *Easy Red (roughly translated)* get to the beach, because the bloody mess floating around was so high that the soldiers couldn't wade through it, and kept sliding around..."

Until this moment I had not given a second thought to how many men had probably become victims of my machine gun fire...

On April 21, 1947 *(the 21st birthday of the then Princess, and present Queen Elisabeth II of England)*, I received the news that I would be released from captivity; my father had applied for my release as a farmer. He would soon be sixty years old and could no longer do the hard work in the barnyard and the fields by himself. So on the 28th of that month I was released to the main camp.

As a prisoner of war in Gosford Camp in Scotland (after returning from the U.S.A. and Belgium - one year before my return to Germany).

On May 20th, along with some others being released, I went aboard the ship that would finally take us back to Germany.

On the afternoon of the next day we arrived in Cuxhaven. There I was loaded on an English truck with some others, and driven to Uelzen, where we were registered at the labor office and received our discharge papers. On the next day, I traveled by railroad from Uelzen to Celle with a comrade *(on the coal tender of the locomotive, which was strictly forbidden)*. There I looked up my brother, Gerhard, and went with him on the same evening on the Celle local to Metzingen, finally back at our farm. I stood there in my *(still)* American work outfit, which looked a bit like civilian clothing, with the large, white prisoner of war identification, the letters PW, on the chest and on the back. This May 22, 1947 was the most beautiful day of my life.

Old Comrades

I had already begun in Scotland, where several thousand men were penned up in a prisoner of war camp, to ask if any of the other prisoners had come from WN 62. I was interested in all that had happened after my departure from my position up at the top of the strongpoint - especially if someone could tell me anything about my battery commander and his death. *(I knew very little of the infantry soldiers of Grenadier Regiment 726 of the 716th Division who were stationed there, as I had only been to the observation post seven or eight times.)* But no matter how often I asked, I could find no one who had been at this strongpoint. It was not until sixteen days later, on the train from Boston to Memphis, that I met someone who had come from WN 62 *(I had just begun my stay in the U.S.A. as a prisoner of war)*. I had asked permission of our *(armed)* American guard to leave the car, and as I walked through the long row of cars, I had inquired in a loud voice if there was anyone here from WN 62. Suddenly, someone had answered, and said that he had been at this strongpoint, in the infantry. Now interested, I asked him how he had got out *(the soldiers had all been in their foxholes on the slope below me, or beside me, and would have had to climb all the way up the hill - past me...)*. He admitted, honestly:

"When I saw that the war was going to erupt right in our sector, my young comrade and I cleared out *(presumably around to the right, down below)* while it was still dark." *(I forgot to ask who the two soldiers were.)*

After the war, and my time as a prisoner of war, I came home after about five years as a different person. The years had left a stamp on me *(not so much the war, but the time as a POW)*. No one had ever spoken to me about my service on June 6, 1944, at WN 62. And I hadn't, out of prudence, spoken a word about it to the Americans... For a long time - at home as well - I kept silent about what I had done then on *Omaha Beach*. Being taken prisoner was a new and painful experience. I had felt, when I was taken prisoner, that it was unfair, had felt myself outlawed and dishonored. It was as if a new life had started at that instant. Until then, there had been an alternative, I could defend myself but then it was over, and everything that had gone before had been in vain. I had then had a feeling of wretchedness, a peculiar, deeply affecting kind of despair, and nothing but interior emptiness...

My parents' house in Metzingen 1933 (in which I still live today)

When I finally returned home after almost exactly three years as a prisoner of war, and altogether almost three and a half years since my last visit in February, 1944, everything seemed different and smaller than before. At first, I felt myself to be a stranger. Half the people in the village were refugees, or people who had lost their houses in the bombings. My parents had also taken in six people, though my attic room was still ready for me. And when I visited old acquaintances in our village, what was

94

frequently said was:

"He isn't back yet..." or "he is still missing..." or "he was killed in action..."

My relationship to my parents was also no longer the same. The disappointments they had experienced in the meantime left them much more reserved about many things. Now, my father went about the affairs that were so important for the maintenance of our farm only halfheartedly. When I made constructive suggestions and said we should do this or that, he often only answered:

"Son, who knows what is still to come..."

My father was frustrated because the Americans, after their arrival, had relieved him of his offices as Bürgermeister *(mayor)* and head of the local farmers' organization of Metzingen, and now he didn't pay much attention to the farm. I watched all this with growing dismay for four weeks, then I said to him, very seriously:

"You know, Papa, I can pack my things up again quickly..."

He must finally have understood that things couldn't keep on this way. I had been granted an early release as a farmer, at his request. *(The son of the farmer, until he has taken over the farm, is known as the vice-farmer. At that time he got his first team of horses and an equal voice with his father in matters concerning the farm.)* In time we succeeded, fortunately, in working it all out.

On the first Sunday following my return home I visited Lisa. We had written each other occasionally over the years, and so she had learned, in the meantime, that I had come home from my confinement. The last time we had seen each other was in March, 1944, three months before the invasion. *(By that time I was already Lt. Frerking's "orderly". When he had gone home on leave to Hanover, he had taken me with him. It was, after all, "necessary" that I deliver his luggage and packages to 23 Friedastrasse..)* Now, after almost exactly three years, Lisa and I finally saw each other again - with consequences. Exactly one year later, on the first day of Pentecost, May 28, 1948, we celebrated our engagement, and another year later, on April 30, 1949, we were married.

At the time, I had been the first to know of the death of my battery commander *(through Kurt Wernecke)*. Frerking had, indeed, been killed in action, but later reported as missing, as his corpse was, until then, untraceable. My parents were now in contact with Frerking's mother, who came to visit us about two weeks after I had returned home *(during the war she had come to our farm a number of times from bomb-damaged Hanover, where there was hardly anything to eat).* She said her son was still reported as missing. I explained to her that I had learned from Kurt Wernecke the location of the place where her son had been killed. It then occurred to us that I should make a sketch of WN 62 and indicate on it the place where her son had been killed, then send this sketch to M. Legrand in Normandy, and ask him to go there to see if there was some sort of improvised gravesite...

Barely two months passed before we had a letter from Legrand. He wrote that he had actually found Bernhard Frerking's place of burial exactly three years to the month after his death. Legrand had found a wooden stake that had been driven perpendicularly into the ground but had, meanwhile, fallen over. Frerking's ID had, at some point, been nailed to it. Then he had reported his discovery to the local authorities, and wrote us a little more than a month later to let us know that Frerking's body had been reburied in the new American military cemetery at Colleville. It had also been ascertained that the lieutenant had been killed *(presumably instantly)* by a shot to his head - as Wernecke had earlier reported.

The Americans had, immediately after the landing on June 6, 1944, created a temporary cemetery for their fallen soldiers on the upper beach, next to the promenade leading from Saint Laurent to Vierville. After the war, a larger military cemetery was developed on the plateau that lay some 55 meters above sea level between Saint Laurent and Colleville. At first, German soldiers were also buried there. In the fifties and early sixties, six German military cemeteries were also established in Normandy, one of them ten kilometers southwest of "Omaha Beach", near the small village of La Cambe.

Six months later, Frau Frerking, who spoke good French and had remained in regular correspondence with Legrand, received the news from him that her son had been reburied once more, and that his final resting place was at the German military cemetery at La Cambe.

I integrated slowly into the everyday life of my hometown, and the distance from *D-Day* grew longer and longer over time. No one asked me about the invasion and the later events, and what had happened up there in Normandy on June 6, 1944. I remained persistently silent... Actually, I had still not come to grips with the terrible and traumatic events on bloody *Omaha Beach.*

Ever since, a single G.I. kept appearing from the horrible images of my dreams, and landed down there on the beach in front of WN 62, and tried to take cover behind the gravel mill. Then I took my rifle, aimed it at him, and shot. His helmet flew through the air and rolled around as if in slow motion, over and over, tumbled over the sand of the beach and was washed out to sea on the falling tide; then the soldier collapsed slowly and fell forward on his face... A few nights later the G.I. appeared on the beach again in my dreams, and again I aimed and shot him, his helmet flew off in a high arc, again he fell on his face, and I shot and he fell... again and again and again...

In the Fifties...

I developed slowly into a loner. I refused to take a position, whether on a political issue, at an organization meeting or a social occasion. "Without me" became an obsession... The cruelty of the war and the knowledge of having followed spurious ideals all dismayed me. And for having done my duty to the end, to wind up a prisoner and be reviled as a "brutal Nazi killer" - the resulting frustration left me more and more taking positions as an outsider, an eccentric *(These eccentric and maverick positions, as well as the reticence, was common to almost all returning veterans)*. I saw no way to work through the experiences of that earlier time, and the more I tried to repress them, the more they ate at me, and the more lonely I felt myself. I felt now that the killing on the beach caused me increasing anguish... Lisa was the only one who displayed any interest in my experiences of June 6, 1944; my parents never asked about it and never learned anything of it. Aside from Lisa, no one knew that,

97

since 1955, and the formation of the new German Federal Armed Forces, I had joined the Association of Conscientious Objectors in Hanover.

Toward the end of 1959, after the first difficult and busy years, I happened one day upon a *(weekly)* installment of a work about the invasion by Paul Carrell, in the magazine, *Kristall,* entitled *Sie Kommen! ("They're Coming!")*. Up until then I had only once seen an article about *D-Day*, and that was during my time as a prisoner of war in the U.S.A.. Now Carrell wrote about many events of June 6, 1944, in his story, including those on *Omaha Beach,* but he omitted any mention at all of the events before and in Colleville, and at WN 62.

By then, I had lost interest in the events of the war, and then I tried to forget about it completely. But, in the meantime, fifteen years had passed, and I had distanced myself from it internally to the point that I shot the G.I. on the beach less and less frequently in my dreams *(at the distance of some years it still happens to me)*. But after almost 37 years I perceived a vague, growing interest in the events of that time, and a growing readiness of my own, finally, to share those things that I had buried so deeply within me, and to work through them. So I wrote to the editors of the magazine *Kristall* and asked why Carrell had written nothing about *Easy Red* and *Fox Green,* in front of Colleville, and about WN 62 since, after all, it was exactly there that the greatest drama of the over 80 kilometer-long invasion coast had played out. Not long thereafter I received a letter from Herr Carrell, in which he asked if I had served there as a soldier and taken part in the fighting. If I were able to tell him anything about the events of that time I should get in touch with him. He had enclosed his telephone number. So I telephoned him, and we arranged that I would call on him at his residence in Hamburg to give an account of June 6, 1944 *(with an appropriate financial compensation offered me)*.

I visited Herr Carell in Hamburg a total of five times in 1960. Paul Carell *(real name Paul Karl Schmidt)* was a likeable man, somewhere in his middle forties *(he died in 1997)*, and I shared for the first time my experiences on the day of the invasion - but about the full extent of what I did then, and the terrible consequences, I still remained silent... Carell, who was at that time working on the book *Sie Kommen!,* asked me to seek out other comrades of that time who could contribute information.

When, during my research, I met old comrades *(one gave me the address of another)* we came, quite casually, to speak of our former "top kick", Sgt. August Wassermeier. I said I assumed that he had been killed on June 6, 1944. To my surprise, I learned, however, that he was quite alive and was working at the courthouse in Brunswick.

At home that evening I talked it over with my wife, who also knew him back then, as she had been taking riding lessons at the same barracks where Wassermeier had served. I said:

"Tomorrow I'm going to Brunswick and visit my old friend..."

The next day, I inquired at the courthouse for the number of Wassermeier's office, and knocked on his door.

"Come in!", I heard him call out, in his old familiar purring tone. I walked in, and there he sat. He had advanced from dairyman to "top kick", to official in charge of traffic violations - but he was no longer wearing as good-looking a uniform ... Across from him, at another desk, sat an older gentleman, a functionary of the old-time sort. I said to Wassermeier:

"Good morning, Herr Wassermeier, I would like to speak with you."

He looked at me; but despite the glasses that had, in the meantime, become necessary, he clearly no longer recognized me:

"Please, what is it then...?

My visit doesn't concern any official business. I have come to you, rather, on a private matter..."

The senior clerk looked up from his papers and said to Wassermeier in a friendly manner:

"Take the gentleman out into the hall..."

Outside, Wassermeier said:

"I don't know you. What do you want of me?"

"Indeed", I replied firmly, "we knew each other during the war. Does the name Wilkening mean nothing to you?" *(I addressed him quite consciously with the familiar "du".)*

He shrugged his shoulders. I reeled off the names of several other non-coms. Then I became more definite:

"On the first day of Christmas, 1943, you had all the 'stable muckers' and 'cribbers' transferred out to 1st Battery...", I said, and counted off for him some names of the people, of which I had also been one.

Wassermeier, who up until then and listened with a furrowed brow, began to nod:

"Yes..., yes"

I said further:

"And I was also such a 'cribber'..."

Now he shook his head:

"Yes, but I don't get it..."

Since he was a few years older than I, and I didn't want to be rude, I asked him:

"May I comfortably continue to address you as "du"?

He nodded forcefully, wanting, obviously, to appear friendly:

"Yes, yes, comrade, naturally!"

"I still remember", I said, "that your name is August. My name is Hein..."

He shook his bowed head again, thoughtfully:

"But I still don't know..."

Then he looked up, and said in a tone as though he were talking of an heroic deed:

"Man, I was lucky then in Normandy. When the shooting started up front, I saddled my horse quickly and was on my way, to the rear, away over the fences.."

The coward had then simply left his people in the lurch, and still seemed to proud of it! But I continued:

"But was there an orderly to Lt. Frerking among your 'cribbers' in the 1st Battery..."

"Yes", he said, "Severloh..."

"You see, August, and I am he..."

"But then you were lucky, too..."

"But you, especially, August, particularly because you were never there where the blows fell and I wasn't there with my rifle..."

He gave me a questioning look:

"Why...?"

"Because I would have loaded my rifle and shot you without hesitation. That would have been the first thing I would have done, if we had encountered each other. I swear I really would have done it."

Startled, Wassermeier moved back a step, and I could see his sudden fear that I might hurt him. But I said, calmingly:

"August, the war is over..."

He stood there and looked at me with confusion. I asked:

"What time do you get off work today?"

"At 5 o'clock", he said hesitantly, but then hurried off:

"It might also be later..."

"Good", I said, "August, I will be back at five, and then we'll go out for a good dinner and some drinks *(the expenses were, after all, for the account of the well-known magazine, "Kristall"),* when we can talk at greater length..."

But Wassermeier rebelled a bit at that:

"Well, I'm not so sure about that...I have to speak to my wife first and ask her..."

Now it was I who reacted:

"What, you have to ask your wife first if you can go with a former comrade from the war when he invites you to dinner...? Well, yes, those who were once big shots are only small fry once they are married..."

Now I had hurt his pride, and he agreed.

A few weeks later there was a meeting I organized among other former comrades I had located in the meantime. We met in Hattorf, near Wolfsburg. Because the original 321st Infantry Division had largely been made up of soldiers recruited from the Brunswick-Magdeburg area, it turned out to be most convenient to meet in the restaurant of another former comrade. I had invited more than twenty men, but in consequence of the border between the two German zones at that time, it was, unfortunately, not possible for the comrades from the then DDR *(Deutsche/German Democratic Republic)* to participate.

When we met then, August Wassermeier also appeared. After I had served everyone a cognac *(the publisher of "Kristall" picked up the tab for this meeting also)* and we had toasted each other, I said:

"And now our great role-model, August Wassermeier gets to shoot off his big mouth. Back then he could do it so well..."

But Wassermeier protested:

"Nooo, I can't do that!"

But after the third cognac his tongue loosened up:

"Imagine what Hein has said to me: if he had caught me there where things were getting hot, he would have killed me..."

To which Karl Rusche, a former sergeant, countered:

"But, August, only if he had been quick enough, because otherwise *I* would have brought you down."

Karl Rusche was a man of his word, and I am certain he would actually have shot the detested Wassermeier. There wasn't one among us who liked Wassermeier, but now we were more inclined to joke about his earlier behavior.

On June 17, 1960, Paul Carell visited me in Metzingen *(not the only time)* and I turned over to him what I had learned from all my former comrades. Carell's book, *Sie Kommen* was supposed to be sent shortly to the printer, and he needed these statements for his account.

I went back to Normandy for the first time in 1961, in order to attend the dedication of the German military cemetery at La Cambe on September 29th. I was very dubious about what awaited me in an encounter with the people there. Besides my wife, I was accompanied by Bernhard Frerking's mother, and his widow, Marie Luise Frerking. I had an odd feeling as soon as I came to the top of the sloping coastal height above *Omaha Beach* and the area of the former Strongpoint WN 62.

After the war, during the construction of the large *(present)* U.S. military cemetery near Colleville, American bulldozers had leveled the area, and filled in the firing trenches and communication trenches. There was no longer anything to be seen of the old, half-buried observation post under the thick overgrowth of blackberry and gorse bushes. It seemed to me that the Americans had tried to erase all signs of WN 62, the strongest German strongpoint on *Omaha Beach,* in front of which such a terrible massacre had played itself out...Only two impressive *(at that time still fenced-in)* monuments to soldiers of the U.S. 1st Division towered over the thick undergrowth; they could only be reached by way of narrow *(also fenced-in)* paths. As I walked slowly through the terrain with the two women I was silent about the location where Bernhard Frerking had been killed - and they didn't ask about it, either... *(Today the area is a single continuous open space, the undergrowth and the en-closures long since removed, the bunkers and machine gun positions uncovered, and the former communication trenches and zig-zag trenches for protection against shrapnel and shell fragments easily observable to a depth of about thirty centimeters.)*

The reunion with Madame and Monsieur Legrand was less depressing. I was greeted like their best friend, embraced and kissed; we hadn't seen each other for more than 17 years, since June 1944. When the Legrands then learned that I was with the three women who had accompanied me, my wife, as well as Frerking's wife and his mother, they were very moved, and said it was to be taken for granted that we should live in the main house of the large Legrand estate for the duration of our stay.

But hardly was that typical French and hearty welcoming ceremony over, when Monsieur Legrand became quite serious and with a pointedly stern face *(which was also somewhat genuine)* led me to the large entrance gate, next to which there was a tall, very sickly looking fir tree

A long expected reunion at the Legrand estate. From left: Bernhard Frerking's mother, my wife Lisa, Madame Legrand and Marie-Luise Frerking. 1ˢᵗ Lt. Frerking had occupied two rooms on the first floor. The room in which I slept as a soldier was behind the large window in the roof.

- with a clear, deep and two hands-wide, large scar *(which had over time grown somewhat higher)...* Fernand Legrand looked at me sternly as he said:

"After your rifle practice on the afternoon of June 5th, about which I learned only later, we didn't see each other again, but this mischief was, unfortunately, not such a good memory of you, Henri..."

He explained to me that he had been particularly proud of this tree, since in the chalky ground of Normandy and the salt sea air, no fir trees actually flourish, and this one was, on that account, the only one in the neighborhood, if not in all of Normandy. Then along came a German soldier and shot it to pieces - just as a joke... I could remember that dull June 5th quite clearly, and that I had cleaned my rifle, and was bored and I was really concerned. Legrand noticed it. He put one hand on my shoulder and silently held out the other to me. A moment later he laughed again.

The mature, though sickly fir tree next to the entrance gate that had grown high since the war must have been cut down shortly after my visit.

After the Legrands had served us a wonderful dinner, Fernand Legrand got up from the table, went to the large, dark cabinet that even at that earlier time had stood in this room, opened a drawer and took out a fountain pen. He put it down on the table in front of Marie-Luise Frerking and said:

"Here, Madame; this pen used to belong to your husband..."

Monsieur Legrand was a large and stylish man *(I had already heard during my time in the military that the people in the area said Legrand was not merely that, but also a "big man")*. His affection for me was greater than his anger over the shot-up fir. We had a long conversation about the former times and my many escapades. I also explained to him that I had bought eggs all around the neighborhood always only one, but that Frerking *(who had not been apprised of it)* and I generally had supplied ourselves from *his* henhouse. Legrand laughed about that and didn't really want to believe it, for it had never occurred to him that there were eggs missing from the nests...

Then I asked Legrand how it had gone with them after Frerking and I had not returned. Fernand Legrand told me that Lt. Frerking, toward 7 o'clock of the morning of June 6[th,] *(the invasion had already begun a half-hour earlier)* had called from the observation post back to the firing position *(at the Battery)* to send a messenger to Legrand's estate to bring Monsieur Legrand to the telephone. Then Frerking advised him and his wife to get into his fast auto and, as a precaution, drive to Bayeux, 10 kilometers further inland, for it was his opinion that this old, historic city certainly would not be fired on by the Germans, and probably also not by the invaders, and that the Legrands would be much safer there for that reason. *(It was not unusual for historic or culturally valuable sites to be excluded from bombing and heavy artillery fire - Bayeux was actually spared throughout.)* The Legrands had then packed their most important things in their car and left the estate. But the American fighter-bombers, which shot at everything on the ground that moved, had also put their journey at great risk. So it seemed then to Legrand more reasonable to turn off to the much shorter stretch of road leading to the firing position of our 1st Battery, and seek cover under the large trees, under which our heavy artillery pieces were also placed. There they waited until late in the afternoon, until the Americans had advanced up to them. Monsieur Legrand also reported that he had witnessed Sgt. Richard Peesel shoot an American scout out of one of the very old, large trees near his estate with the last available howitzer shell. The direct hit, as Legrand explained emotionally, had literally blown the American to bits. After that, the German soldiers had taken leave of Legrand and retreated in the face of the advancing U.S. troops.

In reply to my question as to how the Legrands had got along with the Americans, Fernand Legrand made a disapproving motion with his hand and said, to quote:

"Beaucoup des soldats américains sont des grands cochons..." *(Many of the American soldiers are big pigs.)*

He became excited and angry as he reported further, that the Americans had forced the French women to work for them. Madame Legrand had been made to do laundry for the G.I.'s and to do other work for them things that she left to her maids on her large estate. When she resisted the unfair order of the Americans, one had taken out his pistol and shot at her. Thinking quickly, she had turned and somewhat ducked, so that the shot only grazed her hair.

Sergeants (from left) Alpen and Peesel in front of the company office.

During a long conversation at a restaurant in Port-en-Bessin, before our return to Germany, Monsieur Legrand proposed that I take over his large farmstead and the wide-ranging estate that went with it, as he no longer had any heirs, and he told me the tragic story of his beloved son, who also was named Fernand, and the mysterious circumstances of his death:

On his mother's birthday the son, then just 15 years old, had wanted to bring a rose to the house to give her a little pleasure. While he was picking the rose, he stuck himself with a thorn. At first it seemed completely harmless, but after a few days young Fernand had died - he had been infected by the thorn...

If, considering the initial difficulties with my father after I had returned from my detention as a prisoner of war, I had not found any reason to take over the complete management of our farm in 1953, I would have accepted Legrand's offer immediately. But to manage two large estates

106

- and on top of that separated by over one thousand kilometers - would have been too much for me. So I had to express my sincere regret at having to decline his generous offer, which he also regretted. *(Then, a short time later, Legrand sold his estate.)*

But there was something else that I thought it important to ask Monsieur Legrand during this visit:

When, earlier, in the Spring of '44, I had been billeted at the Legrand estate, there had been an unusually pretty young girl working as a maid at the neighboring farmstead. She was named Suzanne Castell, and was the prettiest girl I had ever seen. We liked each other, but when we met we only would say hello and exchange a friendly smile. Although I felt that I was also attractive to her, and often had the impression that she was only waiting - had I only had the heart to do it - for a word from me to ask her out. On the one hand, I suppose I was worried that she would refuse, and on the other hand it seemed to me it would be a pity if she were to be seen by her countryman as a soldier's girl. *Even though I was sorry about it at the time, I was very happy later about my behavior, for what was done later to French girls who had consorted with German soldiers, after the retreat of the Wehrmacht from France, is well enough known...)*

Now I asked Monsieur Legrand at dinner if he could still remember what had happened to the pretty young maid at the neighboring estate after the war, and how she had managed after that. Monsieur Legrand knew immediately whom I meant, and told me that the young beauty had moved to the - approximately 45 kilometers distant - large city of St. Lô sometime after the war. He didn't know anything further. But while we were still talking Lisa, who had overheard, cut me off and said in Plattdeutsch *(low German)*, and with a soft, indignant undertone, that I had always maintained I had never had a girl in Normandy *(Lisa was, after all, certainly already my girlfriend at that time)*. Now, Madame Legrand had understood. Very forcefully and emphatically she said to Lisa:

"Henri was always proper and had no girl here!"

In connection with one of my visits to Hamburg in 1960, Paul Carell had given me a first edition of the just then published book, "*The Longest Day*". There I read one day about a wave of landing craft of the U.S. 29th Division that had, toward noon, accidentally arrived in my field of fire in *Easy Red* sector, having been thrown off course by the strong current - and what had happened after the soldiers left their landing craft.

It told how the seasick troops, already completely exhausted after the long stay on the troop transports, had then to endure an approach of over twenty kilometers in the landing craft, bouncing over the crests of the waves. Finally, they had to jump into cold water - two meters deep in places - and fight for their lives. David Silva, one of those soldiers, must have been able to tell how many of his comrades right in front of him were shot down as soon as they jumped off the lowered ramp of their landing craft. Then it was his turn to go, and he was immediately pulled under the water by his heavy equipment. When he surfaced, the hail of machine gun bullets hitting all around him in the water created small fountains. In an instant, his knapsack, his mess kit and his uniform were torn up by the machine gun fire. Silva said later that he felt like "a clay pigeon in a shooting gallery", and he could identify the German machine gunner, although he couldn't fire back, as his own weapon was completely jammed by the sand of the beach. At some point Silva had been able to succeed in reaching a shallow mound that stretched the breadth of the area in front of WN 62 *(the embankment about one and a half meters high that separated the tidal beach from the upper beach)* and to take cover behind it. He hadn't noticed until then that he had been wounded in his right leg and back...

Carell had given me two other extremely interesting books at that time; they were *War Histories,* a publication of the U.S. Defense Department, with many illustrations, and the equally detailed, illustrated, *Bloody Omaha.* I learned, coincidentally, from these books about the landing craft described by Silva that had brought him to the beach almost directly in front of my machine gun. The times given, and the description of the place where the boat had landed, coincided exactly with the circumstances I had never forgotten. Since, on June 6, 1944, in our sector, I had the only remaining machine gun, it followed that it was my machine gun that had shot at Silva, and which he could see halfway up the hill from his position on the beach *(especially the conspicuous muzzle flashes, since I was already also firing tracer bullets at that time).* There was not the slightest doubt that I had fired my machine gun at Silva...

In an appendix to *The Longest Day,* I found a section that described what had later become of those *D-Day* soldiers *(by occupation).* It said that David E. Silva was a priest and lived in Akron, Ohio. That awakened my interest in meeting someone who had been my enemy back then, at whom I had shot, and even wounded. So I wrote to the publishing house in New York that had brought out the book, and asked if they could help me find David Silva. I wrote a second letter *(with an incomplete address)* to Mister David Silva, Akron, Ohio, USA...

I never received a reply from the publisher in New York. I waited for months. Instead of that, my letter to David Silva came back *(after almost half a year)*. From what I could gather from the envelope, it had been sent to a total of sixteen*(!)* addresses - always with the notation that the addressee had moved...

My immediate neighbor in Metzingen had an aunt living in the U.S.A., who happened to be visiting him at just the time my letter to Silva was returned. By chance I mentioned this story to her.

The aunt then said that she was flying back to the States in two days, and if I was interested, she would take this letter with her. Naturally, I was interested, particularly because her son worked for the U.S. Defense Department, and she thought he would be able to find out where David Silva was now located. After only little more than two weeks I received a letter from the aunt in America. She told me I could be hopeful that my letter would reach David Silva. Her son had discovered that Silva had rejoined the military. And only two days later she informed me in a further letter that David Silva was now stationed in Karlsruhe as a U.S. Army chaplain....

Already on the next day, May 19, 1963, shortly after midday, my car stood at the gate of the U.S. Army base in Karlsruhe, but I was refused admission. Then the duty officer came over and bent down to the window of my car. I told him my story in general terms, and the reason I wanted to meet Mr. Silva in person. When I then explained to him that I had shot at Silva, a soldier in the U.S. Army, with a machine gun and *(even more to the point!)* had wounded him, the officer took a step back and raised his eyebrows under his helmet. Then his eyelashes fluttered for a moment, obviously very irritated and taken aback by what I had just revealed to him. I added:

"I don't think it would be good for you if I write Mr. Silva, a highly decorated war veteran, that I was turned away from the gate here by the duty officer, when I wanted to visit him..."

The eyelashes fluttered more nervously under the helmet for a long moment - then the duty officer opened the barrier...

David Silva had, in the meantime, received my letter *(from the U.S.A.).* I had written him explaining the strange way in which I had become aware of him, and that I could relate to everything in the American books Paul Carell had given me. Regarding the fact that I had fired at him on June 6, 1944, there was not the slightest doubt. *(Now, I should point out here that front line soldiers of both sides, always and in all wars, respected, even treated each other with esteem when the heat of the battle they engaged in was over: Every soldier also knows that the other didn't cause the war, but only had to follow an order.)*

This is how David Silva looked when I met him for the first time in his office in Karlsruhe: he was then 37 years old and was holding my letter in his hands...

I had been told at the entrance to the base area how to find David Silva's office, and permitted to go there on my own. When I then *(without any advance notice)* entered his office, he sat there in his smart looking uniform and was completely overcome. We had never before knowingly seen each other, and neither had an idea of what the other looked like, but we felt a spontaneous congeniality. We held each other by the arms, clapped each other on the shoulder, and were quite emotional. Our emotions seemed to overflow - just as our eyes... Then we talked until night. We also expressed how incomprehensible it was to us that, in a war, men who are complete strangers shoot at each other - following an order about which they hadn't given a second thought... The soldiers of the other side had the same order, and both parties were armed - another reason to shoot at each other...

When I then asked David how he had come, in the meantime, to be a military chaplain, he explained to me:

"Just when I had to leave the landing craft and encounter your machine gun fire, I called on God to help me get through this Hell alive. I swore that I would become a priest, and as a priest help other soldiers..." *(During the sixties many G.I.'s were shipped out from Germany to Vietnam...)* In this conversation with David Silva it became clear that he had been hit by three of my machine gun bullets.

After I had stayed overnight in his office on a comfortable leather sofa *(the only real problem that presented itself during the night was Silva's cuckoo-clock collection)*, I said goodbye the next morning and drove back to Metzingen - with David Silva's firm promise to visit me and my family at home in the coming weeks.

David Silva (left) visiting at my home.

He came eight days later, and again we were very happy. Silva was a cheerful and humorous person. On his second visit of the year, as I was driving him around and showing him our properties, I suddenly got my car stuck fast in the loose sand of the heath. The rear wheels spun, but the car didn't come loose.

I said to Silva:

"David, start to pray, we're stuck fast..."

Whereupon he answered, calmly:

"No, Hein; before I wear myself out with prayer. I'll gather up my strength and push..."

111

My contact with the Legrands was never again broken. We corresponded frequently. In 1961, Fernand Legrand and his wife even planned to visit us in Metzingen. He wrote on October 22:

Dear Mr. & Mrs. Severloh,

we thank you for your lovely letter, and also for the photos enclosed. It is a joy, after 17 years, to know about each other, and you may be assured that we always think fondly - of the days we spent together.

It may be that we will come to visit you in 1962. It will be up to you to let us know when you expect us. Until we meet, a thousand thanks for your good wishes, and good health to you and your little family.

Fernand Legrand

Unfortunately, nothing more came of this visit. It was put off from year to year by Legrand because of ill health. On May 3, 1964, he wrote:

Dear Mr. & Mrs. Severloh,

We had promised to visit you in the month of May. Now I have, unfortunately, to inform you that I shall have again, for health reasons, to defer this project. I had looked forward to this visit with great pleasure and to seeing you again. I hope, despite this, to see you again, as well as the Frerking ladies, in our country where you left behind a raft of memories.

We hope you are all well, and hope your children are giving you much satisfaction in your old age. We will always be happy to hear from you from time to time.

With our fondest memories, until we meet again,

Fernand Legrand

In December 1972, the news reached me that Fernand Legrand had died on November 24th at the age of 78, news that disturbed me deeply...

In the spring of 1973 Madame Legrand asked me if I could take two young French girls into my house in Metzingen for two weeks. Sixteen year-old Chantal Durand lived in Merville and was a niece of Madame Legrand. She had a friend of the same age named Régine, and the two girls attended high school in Caen. Since they were now also learning German, they wanted to widen their knowledge of Germany. So they came to us in Metzingen.

The two congenial girls, who arrived in August, enjoyed themselves at our house, but the thing they liked the best was the unusual food. They couldn't pass up a fried sausage stand, and helped themselves generously at every meal. It was really a joy to experience these open and nice souls.

At a barbecue on one of our large fields, Chantal drank beer for the first time in her life we had to carry her back to the house that evening...

When the young French girls, who had put on some noticeable pounds, left after two weeks, there was a very affectionate leave-taking... I sent a note for Madame Legrand with them, and a small flower arrangement for Monsieur Legrand's grave.

Only two weeks later, I received a letter from Madame Legrand - already translated into German by Chantal Durand:

Dear Mr. & Mrs. Severloh,

I was very touched by your gesture regarding my husband, which you demonstrated with great sensitivity. I have received your regards through Miss Durand and have immediately put the magnificent flowers on his grave in your name. I don't know how to thank you. He spoke often of the Severloh family, of which he had a very fond memory.

If you can manage it, and come to France next year - and I count firmly on your visit - I will thank you in person. It was a very severe illness that took him from me on November 24, 1972. I have since then remained completely alone here, where as you surely know, we lost our son who I miss as much and I loved him. And then, I have to tell you how painful my loneliness is.

Miss Durand told us what a wonderful reception you gave her. She has an unforgettable memory of the entire family, and that you are surrounded by pretty children, and how completely happy you all seem to be.

A. Legrand

After a further visit in Normandy, in July 1979, during which I was no longer able to locate Madame Legrand *(she was by then in a retirement home in Isigny - about which I was not informed),* a letter from her arrived in August:

Dear Mr. and Mrs. Severloh,

having again found your address through Madame Boher, I want to let you know that I regret that I was away during your visit. I would have been so happy to see you again and to thank you for the flowers that you sent me through Madame d'Allet, and also for the flowers you placed in the cemetery. I was deeply touched by your gesture and am very thankful.

I would have been very happy to see you again and to refresh our memories again. In view of my advanced age (84 years) I do not, un-

113

fortunately, hold out much hope of seeing you once again.
Enclosed is a photo that will certainly please you.
Once again, heartfelt thanks, and my sincere affection - my best
regards.
A. Legrand

One Sunday evening in the spring of 1984, the telephone rang, and it was someone who introduced himself in a friendly way as Franz Gockel, of Hamm/Rhynern. Until that moment I had never heard this name. He explained to me that he had been a soldier in Grenadier-Regiment 726 of the 716th Infantry Division and had been stationed at WN 62. I paid attention immediately and told him that I had also once been up there, but at the observation post. I had only been there a couple of times before *D-Day*, and the observation post was at WN 62 simply as a separate part of the artillery regiment of the 352nd Division. As a result, therefore, I had little to do with the soldiers of the regiment of the 716th Division stationed there, and didn't know the comrades of Gockel's unit. He had become aware of me, as he explained, because he had read about me in Carell's book, "*Sie Kommen!*". We talked for a long time, and, at the end of the telephone conversation, arranged to meet the next day at his home.

On the next day Franz Gockel and his wife greeted me very warmly, and we were immediately congenial. Franz explained to me that he had seen me at WN 62 several times. He had been stationed permanently at the strongpoint for many months and had also "lived" there in the underground troop bunker. Naturally, it attracted the attention of the troops stationed there when we "exotics" from the artillery regiment visited at our observation post. Franz could also remember that I was Lt. Frerking's "orderly". He described to me that, on the morning of the invasion, he had been stationed on an old, water-cooled Polish machine gun in a position improvised from wooden logs, about a hundred meters half-right of my machine-gun dugout, further down the slope and almost at the foot of the hill *(he was at that time only recently 18 years old)*. Then, during the course of the fighting, toward noon, he had been wounded in two fingers of his left hand and had to retreat from WN 62, as the Americans had started to shoot at him, too.

Several weeks later Franz Gockel arranged a meeting with seven other former comrades who, at that time, had been stationed at Strongpoints WN 60, WN 62 and WN 63. He also invited me. From then on, I would see Franz Gockel often in the vicinity of the former strongpoint, there where once we had fought for our lives...

Meeting of former comrades. From left: Franz Gockel, WN 62; Heinz Bongard, WN 60; Bruno Plota, WN 62; Peter Lützen, WN 62; Hein Severloh; Theo Brinkbäumer, WN 62; Hans Selbach, WN 62; Bernhard Lehmkuhl, WN 63 and Michel Schnichels, WN 62.

During my many long visits in Normandy *(after the war)*, I came to know a number of people. There were people from various spheres; journalists, and officials of various committees or agencies, museum directors, private individuals and, of course, veterans of the war.

I had provided a number of artifacts and possessions for exhibition in one of the museums on the invasion coast, the *Musée D-Day Omaha* in Vierville, and spent time at the museum occasionally. Its entire end wall was painted to depict the ocean, with the many warships, the landing craft, and G.I.'s running up the beach. In front of it, a quantity of sand several meters wide had been strewn about to represent the beach. On this "beach", steel obstacles had been placed and barbed wire entanglements laid down. Two German soldiers *(mannequins)* in uniforms and helmets crouched down in a "Tobruk" position in front of the barbed wire behind an MG 42, and on an explanatory label in front of it was written: t*he Pfc.'s Franz Gockel and Hein Severloh*. I had to laugh out loud, when I read this label and saw the two "puppet comrades".

The director of this museum, Monsieur Leveel, introduced me to an

115

American by the name of Jack Borman. Borman wore a light, sand-colored tropical outfit, horn-rimmed glasses and a "southwester" hat, whose wide brim was fastened up on one side. He was a reserved, un-assuming active man, accompanied by another American. In conversation with Jack Borman and Monsieur Leveel, it emerged that on June 6, 1944, Borman, a soldier in an armored unit, had landed in my sector *(Easy Red)* in a tank fitted for amphibious operation *(Sherman Duplex Drive)*. The man accompanying Borman said that Jack had harbored real feelings of remorse ever since then because he had fired on the German strongpoint. Borman looked at me and said, softly:

"Yes, I was a tank gunner and destroyed an artillery piece in your position..."

The other said, further:

"Jack has worried about that seriously for forty years, thinking he might have wounded, or even killed a German soldier with that round...I advised him, long ago, to fly over to one of the anniversaries in Normandy and to meet with Germans there, to talk with them, and to ask if they bore him any ill will for having shot at them back then..."

When I heard that, I had to smile. Then I took Jack by the shoulders and said:

"Do you think, Jack, that we liked doing what we had to do? We know also that you were as reluctant as we. None of us could have done anything differently..."

Jack still had vague doubts:

"And your people are not angry with me...?"

I shook my head, and Jack's expression brightened.

Then Jack Borman told me about his experiences. He was in the crew of the tank that, during the morning of June 6th, down there in front of the entrance to the valley leading to Colleville, had become stuck in the steep gravel and been unable to maneuver. *(This tank can be seen in various books about "D-Day"; Adolf Schiller spent the night of June 6/7 hidden in it.)* At some point he had delivered the single shot at the higher of the two casemates of WN 62. Then the tank crew decided it would be better, in their hopeless situation, to remain completely passive. So the tank remained motionless in the middle of the terrible fighting, and no one - neither the one side nor the other - took any serious notice of it. The troops in it could follow the fighting around it through the observation slit, and were very much afraid for their lives. Only as darkness fell did they finally risk leaving the tank...

Since we became acquainted at the museum in Vierville, Jack Borman has been back at every anniversary on *Omaha Beach*... Many other men whom I later met, who were my "enemy" during the war, became my lifelong good friends.

With Jack Borman (right), ex-tank gunner with remorse, at the German military cemetery at La Cambe.

Heroes are Out

During the Second World War, the German soldier had, for propaganda purposes, been surrounded by an heroic aura, made into the defiant old soldier, girded with an ideologically charged and mystically intensified fighting spirit (*every veteran soldier an angel of death...*). Heroes fitted precisely into the picture of the time. But times have changed in the more than half-century since; today heroes are *out* - but not everyone seems to have comprehended that...

On the occasion of my visit to *Omaha Beach* in 1984, on the 40th anniversary of the invasion, I was approached by two families from the Black Forest at the former WN 62. They explained that they were interested in the historical events of that time, had already read a great deal about me, and that I was a genuine hero in their eyes. We walked here

The large U.S. cemetery on the heights in front of Colleville, containing 9,286 graves, in 1953. On the upper left of the picture is the area of WN 62 (white outline). When I visited this cemetery for the first time, I was deeply affected. (1 = U.S. 1stDivision monument; 2 = U.S. Engineer monument; 3 = my machine-gun position with my field of fire (between the arrows).

and there around the slope of the hill for some time, and I answered the questions they put to me. Over time, during the many visits to the area, I noticed two men who lingered near us more and more frequently, and who wandered about in the uniform of the American 101st Airborne Division. After the family from the Black Forest had left, the two spoke to me. They had, by then, understood from my comments that I had once been a member of the 352nd Infantry Division. They introduced themselves and explained to me that they were Englishmen, and belonged to the *World War II Re-Enactment Association, Ltd.* in Great Britain. They told me their association stood for the rehabilitation of the honor of the German soldiers of the Second World War, and they wished to invite me to the ceremony in connection with the formation of "their" Infantry Regiment 916, on November 16th *(1984)*. In answer to my question as to why they would go around on *Omaha Beach* in uniforms of American paratroopers, they told me it was the only acceptable alternative to

German Wehrmacht uniforms that presented itself *(on the invasion coast it is forbidden for anyone - neither veterans nor others - publicly to wear the Wehrmacht uniform)*. I didn't want to ask why they didn't want, rather, to wear English uniforms...

On November 16, 1984, I flew to England, to the *Association for the Rehabilitation of the Honor of the German Wehrmacht Soldiers*. The association had, meanwhile, written me in Germany, and I was interested in what was going on with them. When I arrived at the London airport, I was astounded. A member of this curious association was waiting for me there with a car, dressed *(quite publicly)* in a German Wehrmacht uniform of a simple private first class *(but without a service cap)*. A silver Infantry Assault Badge *(it had been awarded, since 1939, to seasoned infantrymen who had participated in at least three front-line assaults on three separate days of combat)* was displayed on his uniform, and a gold Close-Combat Badge *(awarded, since 1942, to soldiers who had proven themselves in at least 50 days of close-combat)*. I had known that in England *(and also in the U.S.A.)*, there were associations whose members dressed as members of the German Wehrmacht, play-acted with rifles and machine guns, and drove around in old German cars *(and were even covered on television and in the press)*, but it had not been at all clear to me until my meeting with this club what these activities were. But I had no idea how awful it was to become...

In the VW-Kübelwagen *(VW-jeep)* that picked me up, there was another man, who introduced himself as F....W.... and wore civilian clothes. He spoke fluent German, and explained to me that he was a former German citizen, served as a soldier in the war, and was taken prisoner by the English. He had stayed in Great Britain after the war and taken a new name. After a short ride in the car, he had the "Pfc" stop, excused himself for a moment, took a large bag from the back seat and disappeared into a public toilet - in the middle of the city. After a while, the vehicle door was opened and Mr. W. got in again - now in the smart uniform of a German captain of the Wehrmacht. His jacket was decorated with an EK-II-ribbon *(Iron Cross, 2nd Class; it was a black-white-red ribbon worn in the second buttonhole)*, an EK I *(Iron Cross, 1st Class; awarded for "exceptional bravery in the face of the enemy")*, a silver Infantry Assault Badge, a black Wound Badge *(awarded from September 1, 1939, on the model of that of the First World War, to persons wounded once or twice by enemy weaponry)*, and a clasp with a number of service decorations. I had fallen in with a circle of great heroes...

A little later we entered the meeting room of this dubious association. A "lieutenant" in a dress uniform with a parade sash (instead of a belt) and a sword with a knot at the hilt, shouted, "Attention!". At his command, twenty men sprang from their chairs and stood at attention. Then another command:

"In honor of Pfc. Hein Severloh, present arms!"

And other "soldiers" in helmets, formed up in two ranks, presented arms. It seemed to me that I had been caught up in the midst of the pieces of a military museum come to life.

"Present arms - Hein Severloh arrives!" Of all the nonsense related to D-Day I had experienced, the business with this "Association" on the occasion of my visit was, without doubt, the greatest.

At a long table that formed a large, closed rectangle, stood uniformed Englishmen in Wehrmacht uniforms bedecked with decorations. In the middle of this rectangle there was a table on which there were two German rifles, Type 98k, and an MG 42. In two corners of the hall various, large German battle flags with swastikas and iron crosses were draped, and on the table there were quantities of beer bottles. This was the moment when I should have turned and left, but my curiosity to see what would happen next was greater.

Another "officer" came forwarded and saluted me, then saluted the "captain", who returned the salute, and then there was much saluting to give the whole thing a smart, disciplined and German military character. The seat to which I was shown, in the middle of one of the ends of the rectangular table, was marked by a two meter-high and one-and-a-half meter wide board that had been adorned with the Wehrmacht insignia and the insignia of my former division. Above, in large letters, was written *352nd Infantry Grenadier Division*, and underneath *(erroneously)* three Hitler Youth bicycle pennants. The "officers" of the Association took their places next to me. The "lieutenant" noticed that I could barely suppress a laugh, and asked me in an offended undertone:

"Tell me, are you laughing at us?"

"No, Herr Lieutenant", I replied, "I am simply imagining that when I return to Germany and explain what I experienced here, no one will believe me..."

There was a long and nonsensical speech, then I was asked how it had gone back then, on *D-Day* at WN 62, and I saw that I was being asked to make some remarks. After which I was to give the "Wehrmacht comrades", in their waxworks, an explanation of the functioning of the machine gun, Model 1942. But I refused that firmly since, from the moment on the afternoon of June 6th, 1944, when I had thrown my machine gun into the blackberry bramble up there on the hill in front of Colleville, I was no longer prepared to take hold of such a terrible killing machine ever again in my life.

Then came the highpoint of this dubious performance. The English "Wehrmacht comrades" had read in some or another books or magazines that I had been wounded twice on June 6, 1944, and since, on account of my imprisonment I had never received a wound badge, they would award it to me now. It was hardly to be believed, but I actually received a small carton with the black decoration and, with it, an "original" award document; in the name of the Führer and the Supreme Commander of the Wehrmacht - signed by F.W., self-appointed *Captain and Company Commander of Grenadier Regiment 916 of the 352nd Infantry Division.* The document bore the date, *In the Field, June 6, 1944* and was stamped with a seal of the 352nd Infantry Division, with an Imperial Eagle and Swastika...

Before my return to Germany, on the next day we all visited the Invasion Museum in Portsmouth that had been dedicated by the British Queen on June 6, 1984. The members proudly wore the insignia of the 352nd Division on their shirts - they really believed they were an elite unit,

Im Namen des Führers und Obersten Befehlshabers der Wehrmacht
verleihe ich dem

Gefreiter Heinrich S E V E R L O H

das

Verwundeten Abzeichen

Im Feld, den
6. Juni 1944

Hauptmann u. Komp.führer

The original Wound Badge of the German Wehrmacht awarded to me, together with the accompanying award document - and all in the name of the "Führer":
"In the name of the Führer and the Commander-in-Chief of the Wehrmacht, I award to Private First Class Heinrich Severloh the Wound Badge. In the field, June 6, 1944"

as the division was constantly described incorrectly by the Americans...

When I was flying back to Germany I asked myself if these people actually were really were clear about what they were doing. Quite clearly they had not grasped at all that we had then been following false ideals that had plunged our entire world into a terrible catastrophe.

Whatever attitude an individual takes toward the Third Reich, the Wehrmacht and the war is solely his own completely personal affair. I don't mind if he thinks he has to play at being a Wehrmacht soldier, for I am not writing this book to moralize, but rather to describe my own very personal experiences. What a reader draws from my account and my completely subjective approach is also completely up to him. But per-

haps a Wehrmacht re-enactor would think differently had he done what I did and seen what I saw then...

As I looked down at the French coast from the airplane, I remembered that I had once been somewhere down there behind my machine gun trying to defend my life. I was, certainly, not the only German soldier who fired down from the strongpoints at the invading Americans, but it can't be ruled out that I was *the* soldier of the Second World War who had with my firing put the most opposing soldiers out of action, and this fact is for me the saddest thing in the world - and with this in mind, I definitely do not feel like a hero. It would have been bad enough if I had only wounded a single one of them. I didn't know any of the G.I.'s, and they didn't know me, but we had fired at each other then, since we had been ordered to do it...

If you read Paul Carell's book, *Sie Kommen!* you might easily get the impression that there were not many people at our strongpoint besides Frerking and me. In a drawing of *Omaha Beach* from this book, the position is labeled *WN 62 1ˢᵗ/352 (Severloh)* and appears almost as if I had been the commander of this strongpoint. In many other books, also, Frerking and I came to be depicted as some sort of heroes of the Third Reich. *(It would be futile to try to list all the titles of books that refer to me; there could be no complete listing as I am not aware of all the books.)* The worst *(heroic)* nonsense that I have found written about me appears in the book, *Vorwärts! Omaha Beach 6. Juni 1944* by the French authors Laurent Mari and Jean-Jacques Gaffié, published first in 1994, in the forward of which Gilles Perrault also wrote:

"...fifty years later we have here the newest and most absorbing summing-up of the battle on *Bloody Omaha."*

In the book it says *(to quote):*

"...Severloh can see clearly how the gun turrets of the USS Emmons turn toward WN 62 *(I have never heard of the ship).* The shells landed around him. His machine gun is knocked over three times, but still works. He gives his all. Since the usual ammunition has been exhausted, he is forced to use tracer bullets which, however, reveal his position. Devil take it! He is resolute to the end..."

In another chapter is written:

"Heinrich Severloh doesn't want to be hit. His machine gun still spreads death. Destroyer shells land just right of him three times. His trench has, for the most part, collapsed. But he resumes the fight each time. All Germany stands behind him(*!*). He feels it deep in his heart. It is his duty as a soldier. It is almost as if the whole armada has come solely to destroy him - him, the young farmer's son from Metzingen..."

And further, in another place:

"...His ammunition was as good as exhausted. Severloh succeeded in withdrawing to Captain Frerking's *(Germanization of the French Capitaine=Hauptmann, but Frerking was "only" a 1ˢᵗ Lieutenant)* bunker, where he came across two fire control officers who were panic stricken. One of them moaned,

"We're finished!"

Eberhard Schulz, a friend of Severloh *(I have never had a friend or comrade by that name)*muttered:

"Do me a favor and take him away, he's driving me crazy with his panicky behavior"

Severloh took the officer by the collar *(in this erroneous mix-up, clearly it was Sgt. Beermann who was meant, and not an officer; besides which, neither of the two fire control officers, 1ˢᵗ Lt. Frerking and Lt. Grass, had acted panicky):*

"You want to fight? You want to shoot? Now the time has come!"

The frightened officer bowed his head. Severloh gripped him more firmly and dragged him out of the small bunker *(Beermann had always wanted very much to fire my machine gun).* Heinrich showed him his machine gun, a few meters away, and said:

"You see that? Now listen well to me. You have only one try. Put your finger on the trigger and pull it as soon as you can see over the parapet. Do it quickly, as they will get you as soon as they see your helmet. Fire one round and then duck, otherwise you are dead. Come on!"

The officer hurried forward and managed to get off a couple of rounds *(what is meant is bursts)* before the trench was hit by a shell. Severloh ran to him through the hail of bullets. The man and the machine gun were buried *(at our position no one was buried alive - even Beermann).* He dug for him with his bare hands. The poor officer was still breathing, but is completely paralyzed. Severloh urged him on:

"Go, get up, this is the end of the road."

There were only fifty rounds left in his MG 42. Captain Frerking left the bunker. He gave the order to retreat. A shell came through the observation slit of the bunker *(the shell hit the upper edge of the observation slit).* The earth shook. The tanks and destroyers of the allies made an end of WN 62. In a period of eight hours *(actually nine hours)* Severloh fired ten thousand bullets *(in fact it was 12,500 rounds)*. Because of his marks-manship one can easily count up how many G.I.'s he killed. Severloh shook his Captain's hand, took his machine gun, and went on his way. Frerking is dead. Officer Pie is dead *(Pie was only a master sergeant and, though wounded, had survived the 6th of June)*. Only three of the soldiers on the hill survive: Severloh, Gockel and a young radioman *(Wernecke)."* *(Besides the three mentioned above, of the total of 41 of soldiers sta-tioned at WN 62, the following survived on June 6th: Sgt. Förster, the Cpl.'s Krieftewirth, Brinkmeier, Brinkbäumer, Kuska, Lützen and the Pfc.'s Flossmann, Kowalski, Kwiatkowski, Selbach, Schnichels, Bersik, as well as Pfc. Plota and Pvt. Heckmann - the fate of several others remains unknown.)*

About this "newest and most absorbing summing-up of the battle" one can only shake his head in astonishment...

At the end of 1999, I saw the film, *"Saving Private Ryan"*. For a long time, I tried to avoid it, and had heard about the horrific scenes of the landing on the beach... Certainly, what I saw in the film seemed horribly familiar to me, and I believe it depicts accurately what happened down there on the beach; the tension of the G.I.'s when the ramps of the landing craft fell, then the awful hail of bullets, the falling artillery shells, scatter-ing body parts, bodies ripped to pieces, blood on blood the dreadful screams of the wounded, the frenzy of fear and the agonizing, almost endless distance to the upper beach...

The photography and the special effects of this film are, without doubt, a technical tour de force, and present, in my opinion, very realisti-cally, the real horror that had taken place on the beach. At that time, however, I had observed the events from a completely different point of view. In the beginning, I saw the events from a distance of 600 meters and, after the tide had risen, still from roughly 150 meters, and from a different perspective - often between frequent thick clouds of dense, black smoke and the occasional spouting of fountains of earth from the targeted rounds of naval artillery. I saw how the G.I.'s - who in the stress of it all were not more than anonymous creatures to me - ran around down there, and I fired among them with my machine gun. I shot at *attackers*, of whom it had been said, they were my enemies. Since I was also being shot at, I felt my actions at that moment to be completely natural. Be-sides which, I had no time at all to reflect on it, as I had also fallen into an apocalypse. There were no logical thoughts then, everything moved as if in a swirling nightmare...

When I see these scenes today, I get noticeable palpitations, and it touches me deeply. I feel a great sympathy for the GI.'s who were brought over from America to a coast of which they knew nothing, then to die a miserable death there. It is only when one grows older that he knows youth should be cherished, and these men were all young...

In many interviews, I have tried to emphasize the real tragedy of those events, to make my account somewhat pedagogical to wake people up. But I have to conclude that in the end, people had always wanted to make sensational stories out of my account, with fame and heroism. But I ask myself how anyone can be a hero when he has killed men...

With the author, Helmut Konrad von Keusgen, on the beach in front of the former strongpoint 62. Here, on June 6, 1944, lay the corpses of hundreds of GI.'s and countless dying and wounded. Von Keusgen, who has visited this beach for thirty years and spent a number of years in Normandy, often asked who these men were who had manned the German machine guns. My meeting with him, and our work together on this book have created a close bond, and I don't think there is anyone who had not been here at the time who can understand as well as he what we experienced here. I was able, in our many conversations, almost sixty years later, to acquire new insights, and to understand myself better in many ways.

126

In the forty years during which I have been interviewed so often, no one has ever asked me if, today, I would still fire at the GI.'s on the beach. The author, Helmut Konrad Baron von Keusgen, was the first to put this question to me, in May, 2000, in connection with his research for his book, *"D-Day 1944 - The Allied Landing in Normandy"*, as we stood at the place on *Omaha Beach* where once my machine gun had been. I felt it a difficult question, and very serious, so he gave me some time to think about it. Then I answered him:

"Today, and bearing in mind the experience of that time, I would go down to the beach to meet the Americans and wait to see what would happen then. But I would never shoot again - even if I knew I would be hit by their bullets. But now I am an old man..."

What I do not, however, find to be good in Spielberg's film, *"Saving Private Ryan"*, is *(as is often the case in American films)* the explicit anti-German bias, in which the German soldiers are often portrayed as fanatical Nazi's, cruel beasts and sub-humans. *(Even the newer books there still write of the "enemy".)* And it is just this bias that makes it so difficult for people to meet without preconceptions. Times have changed by now, and also the mindset of people. Then we were indoctrinated with patriotism; today, finally, people think more liberally.

If nothing has been learned from what once took place on *Omaha Beach* on June 6, 1944, on behalf of freedom and humanity, then the poor G.I.'s down there died in vain...

Publicity

When Paul Carell wrote about me and Strongpoint WN 62 in 1960, in his book, *"They're Coming"*, that was the first step toward a celebrity such as I never could have imagined. I would still have led the simple, orderly life of a farmer, like so many others - if it had not been for that one day in my life, this June 6, 1944...

On the occasion of the dedication of the German military cemetery at La Cambe and the ceremonies in connection with it, in September, 1961, I didn't only visit the graves of comrades killed in action, but also again met some of the survivors of *D-Day*. There were some others, as well as veterans of the war, who had read Carell's book, and knew by that time who I was. Even on this first visit to Normandy after the war, many reporters spoke with me at the cemetery. How they found out so quickly who I was *(and among the huge crowd of participants in the ceremonies)* always remained a mystery to me. But it seemed to me there, already, that I was like the famous "spotted dog" in the German children's story, who stood out from among all the other monochrome animals colored only in shades of gray. I gave many interviews, the consequence of which was that more and more journalists sought me out. After the universally acclaimed book, *"The Longest Day"*, by Cornelius Ryan, Carell's *"They're Coming"*, and a number of other books, it seemed there was almost a *D-Day-Boom*, for the interviews *(later also at my home)* increased significantly in the sixties. I received inquiries from many parts of the world; as, for instance, from an American university in Los Angeles. A multi-part series in the Belgian military journal, VOX, and books in German, English and French wrote about the soldier, Hein Severloh, at WN 62 on *Omaha Beach*.

"BLOODY OMAHA" (IV)

Alarm, ze zijn daar !

In februari '44 bevond korporaal Heinrich Severloh, toen twintig jaar, zich in Normandië met de 352ste divisie onder het bevel van generaal Krais. Deze 352ste divisie was gevormd uit de resten van de 311de divisie, die in Rusland gehalveerd was.

De 352ste divisie was samengesteld uit drie infanterieregimenten en één artilleriebataljon. Het 352ste artilleriebataljon telde drie lichte artilleriebatterijen uitgerust met 105 mm kanonnen en één zware batterij met 150 mm kanonnen.

Elke batterij telde 120 manschappen : officieren, onderofficieren en soldaten ; tussen die 120 waren er 15 vrijwilligers "Hilfwillige". Vaak ging het hier om soldaten uit de huidige oostbloklanden die gevangen genomen waren en ingelijfd in de Duitse Strijdkrachten waar, zoals het Duitse begrip het zegt, ze de strijders hielpen. Soms waren ze zelfs niet gewapend.

In de 716de divisie, waarvan de Amerikanen dachten dat ze de enige was in de Omaha-sector, bevonden er zich bijvoorbeeld hele regimenten vreemdelingen, waarvan de onderofficieren, korporaals en soldaten Oekraïners waren, maar de hogere kaders Duitsers.

Verbonden aan het 352ste rijdende

De kapitein en hijzelf logeerden bij Mr. en Mevr. Legrand te Houtteville. Ieder beschikte over een zeer comfortabele mansardekamer in de ruime woning van deze vriende'ijke mensen. Op een goeie afstand hiervan, in een grote wei, had men de vier 105 mm kanonnen geïnstalleerd van de 1ste batterij van het 352ste.

Severloh voelde zich goed thuis te Houtteville, een gehucht van Surrain dichtbij Trévières. Hij beschouwde de Legrands een beetje als zijn ouders en hij voelde veel respect en sympathie voor hen.

In het Duitse leger, waar de discipline erg streng was, was het verboden dat de Duitse soldaten vriendschappelijk omgingen met de Franse bevolking. Dit belette korporaal Severloh en 1ste luitenant Frerking niet lange gesprekken met Mr. en Mevr. Legrand aan te knopen over de boerderij en de gewassen.

Mr. Legrand had in 1914 nog in de loopgraven gevochten en hij had er zelfs een litteken van een schrapnel in de schouder aan overgehouden ; hij rakelde dan ook herinneringen aan de "grote oorlog" op, 's avonds bij een glas cider of calvados.

Ja, Severloh voelde zich erg in zijn sas bij de Legrands. Hij hield van Normandië, een streek die hem aan zijn dorp deed

KORPORAAL SEVERLOH (20 J), EEN VAN DE SOLDATEN DIE OP 6 JUNI 44 OMAHA BEACH VERDEDIGDEN.

Dank zij zijn sterke gestel kwam hij er weer bovenop. De talrijke herstelverloven die hij doorbracht in het gezellig buitenverblijf van de Severloh's te Metzingen-über-Celle, hielpen hem weer op de been. In Metzingen ontmoette hij Elisabeth Schliephake en het was liefde op het eerste gezicht. Hand in hand wandelden beide verliefden in de mooie, natuurrijke omgeving. (*)

Mooie liedjes duren echter niet lang. Na talrijke vergunningen, kwam de dag dat de jonge korporaal, helemaal genezen,

In 1982, the Belgian military journal, "VOX Military Weekly" covered me again (they had already published my story in the sixties; again this time, unfortunately, without my hoped-for emphasis that killing is something awful - even for soldiers).

The dedication ceremony of the cemetery seemed strange, almost bizarre, due to the unusual circumstance that the many visitors, during the speeches and the laying of wreathes, were able to hear constant sounds of battle from the distant coast. The thunder of artillery fire rumbled from far away. It seemed as though the 6th of June, 1944, wanted to mark this reverent and ceremonial day and remind us once again of the difficult hours and the suffering it had brought to so many people. The distant, sinister rumbling of the war communicated more than the many words of the officials. As I learned after the ceremonies, there was on that same day, extensive filming of *"The Longest Day"*, in Port-en-Bessin, 26 kilometers distant, on the coast...

After this first, impressive visit in Normandy, I visited the French west coast again for many anniversaries of *D-Day*. Over time, the interviews and the resulting publicity grew noticeably, and more and more often I met former soldiers of the other side.

One day in 1975, I received a letter from the French television corporation, RTF *(Radio and Television France)* in Paris, from a Ms. Schick *(a German who was an interpreter at this TV station)*. She informed me in the letter that a documentary film was being planned, with the title *Le Grand Jour (The Great Day)*, and offered a generous payment for my assistance. I accepted, and flew *(with my wife)* to Paris, and traveled from there by train to Normandy. We were to be in the former invasion area for two weeks. Two well-known Englishmen, John Howard and Terence Otway, were also brought to Normandy for the filming.

John Howard, then a major, led the successful "coup-de-main" to take the Pegasus Bridge over the Orne-Caen canal, and Terence Otway, then a 1st lieutenant, led a simultaneous "coup-de-main" that was supposed to take the German coastal battery at Merville, on the furthest left flank of the allied invasion; but this attack by the English developed into a terrible disaster.

Aside from one French veteran and another former German soldier, there was also an American veteran at the filming. The American had stayed in Normandy after the war, married the daughter of a French farmer, and taken over the farmstead immediately behind WN 62. Later, however, he had divorced the French wife and returned to the U.S.A. *(that had not improved his image with the French)*. For the film, I was to walk from the site of the former strongpoint up to the U.S. military cemetery, in conversation with this American who had landed back then in the hail of my bullets. When I asked the director, later, why there was only a single American at the filming, he answered:

"One American is enough for us..."

The filming of *"Le Grand Jour"* took place at a number of venues, in different places. In the course of it we were in Sainte-Mére-Église, Carentan, at *Utah Beach,* at Pegasus Bridge, in Merville and other historic places. On the first evening, we all went, including the two congenial Englishmen, Howard and Otway, to a restaurant in Carentan for our dinner, where we sat *(with our wives)* at several tables. When the two Englishmen noticed that all the former soldiers of the various countries were separated, Otway said:

"We insist that we all sit together at one table..."

In the late spring of 1984, I received a letter *(with another lucrative offer)* from the large Norman daily newspaper, *Ouest France*, in which I was asked to report on the 40th anniversary. They even offered to send a private airplane to get me, but I preferred to go via commercial airline to Paris; a reporter from the paper picked me up there during the night. We arrived in Normandy at dawn, where a group of the editorial staff and an interpreter awaited me. For three long days *(from May 11th to May 13th)*, together with five American veterans *(at whom I had fired from WN 62 on June 6, 1944)*, I was interviewed extensively at the site of the former strongpoint. All were very relaxed and friendly, except for a former general who could not forgive me for having once fired at him and made the advance on the beach so difficult. The rest of us got along well together. On June 6th of that year, exactly on the date of the anniversary, a long article appeared on the first page of *Ouest France,* under the headline, *They Were Enemies at Omaha...* with a number of photos, some in large format. The article also carried a detailed account of my visit to old Madame Legrand in a retirement home in Isigny-sur-Mer. She had, by then, become almost blind. *(It was the last time I saw Madame Legrand; she died in May, 1986, at the age of 92.)*

During the course of my visit in Normandy, journalists kept approaching me, even a reporter from Finland took an interest in my story. The general carnival atmosphere on the occasion of this 40th anniversary was indescribable, and with regard to me, I had the impression that one reporter gave my name to the next, and then I was constantly accosted. The outer boundary of sorrow was reached then at the German military cemetery at La Cambe. On the occasion of the *(very elaborate)* memorial commemoration there, a sixty man-strong *(French)* military chorus sang *Ich hatte einen Kameraden (I had a comrade)*. In this moment of deepest emotion, an American television reporter leapt out next to me from the silent, reverent crowd and tried to interview me. It was as if I had been hit in the head...

A remarkable position: surrounded by the men at whom I had fired my machine gun at this exact point on June 6, 1944, I stood in front of the cameras of the reporters. The man with the hat is a former American general who was friendly neither to his former subordinates nor to the French - but he was the most unfriendly to me.

On the afternoon of June 5th, the day before the 40th anniversary, I left my car in the parking lot above the former WN 62. I took my walking cane out of the car *(it was a special cane; when the point was set in the ground, it could be opened, and a wide leather strap provided a comfortable place to sit)*. I almost lost my temper when I was addressed in English. Out of the crowd of visitors who come here on the anniversaries, particularly in this section of the invasion coast, two Americans, somewhat older than I, came toward me. One of them pointed to my walking stick and said:

"I like that. Sell it to me. I will give you a dollar for it."

"A hundred dollars", I replied glibly.

He was shocked:

"But that would be fleecing me..."

To which I countered:

"And at one dollar you would be fleecing me..."

Since we were headed in the direction of the site of WN 62, we fell into conversation. The Americans asked me who I was and what I was doing here. I said that I am a German and had come to look around at everything. Actually, however, it was because Franz Gockel had arranged a meeting *(including me)* for an extensive interview at the site of the strongpoint with several reporters from the magazine, *Bunte*.

The two Americans now explained that they had been members of the 16th U.S. Infantry Regiment of the 1st Division at the time, and had landed right in front of this German strongpoint in a hellish hail of bullets. Meanwhile, we arrived at the place from which I had fired on the beach on June 6, 1944 - and now I told them that. They were flustered for a moment, then one of them said, smiling:

"You damned pig..."

Then he explained to me:

"After we had finally got up down here *(at the point where the upper beach rose one-and-a-half meters over the tidal beach),* there were only 24 men left of our 250 man-strong battalion who were not wounded or killed... All our 16 officers were either dead or wounded; a sergeant had to take over command of the remainder of the company. The two of us *(he pointed at his comrade)* were captains at the time, and we, too, were wounded."

For the reporters from *Bunte*, this accidental meeting - Franz Gockel and I, with the two passing Americans - was a sensational story, but they couldn't resist shaking their heads at what they heard from us...

At this time, several reporters of the U.S. television network, ABC *(American Broadcasting Corporation)* became aware of me. They persuaded me to do an interview at the former WN 62 *(the interview lasted over four hours, and was broadcast as a one hour program in the U.S.A. on June 6th).* I noticed during the interview that they were well prepared and had already informed themselves about me and about my story which, by then, had appeared in additional books *(in the U.S.A. as well).* I was asked direct questions, to which I gave honest and detailed answers. I had long since brought myself to the point of being able to talk about *(almost)* everything. At the end of the program, the reporter, in front of the still-running camera:

"So, Mister Severloh, now I still have three questions: First, who, at that time, gave you the order to shoot?"

This question confused me somewhat. I shrugged my shoulders:

"No one told me to do that...", I answered frankly, and added, truthfully:

"...I was merely told beforehand to open fire when the G.I.'s were still in knee-deep water; they wouldn't be able to spread out..."

The reporter nodded and asked his second question:

"Couldn't you have run away rather than shooting?"

I had never thought about that. I was a soldier, and foreign troops were landing down there, who we regarded, logically in our situation, as enemies - who were armed to the teeth in order, if it had been possible, to kill *me* as well - and my machine gun had been placed here... For me, the thought of running away had never occurred, and I said so to the reporter, and added:

"I would not have run away in any case. To leave my comrades in the lurch would, for me, have been the worst thing I could have done in this situation. I would have had to live the rest of my life as a coward..."

Then the reporter asked his last question:

"Mister Severloh, how many men did you take down on the beach down there?"

This question came at me like the crack of a whip. The reporter had, in his insolent way, found my most sensitive spot. First I tried to dodge the question:

"That I don't know, there was no one to count..."

But he didn't give up:

"Then, roughly..."

I tried again to leave the question unanswered:

"I have no idea..."

He bored in further:

"Was it more than a thousand...?

Now it was too much for me, and because it affected me so disagreeably, I took an equally insolent attitude and replied brusquely:

"It was certainly more than one thousand - more than likely more than two thousand men.."

Now it was out in the open, that which weighed so heavily on me for almost forty years to the day - that which I had carried with me in secret and which I thought I never would be able to express. From then on, I felt, in some inexplicable way, relieved, and it no longer felt difficult to talk of the events of that former time quite openly. I continued to be interviewed frequently, and as time went by, sundry newspaper articles, magazine and book accounts, as well as television programs appeared, but in reply to the question of how many soldiers I had brought down on June 6, 1944, for a long time I gave no further answer, and also didn't want to travel to Normandy ever again. Sixteen long years went by before I was finally ready to really talk of *everything*...

My last visit with Madame Legrand, who had by then become completely blind, in a retirement home in Isigny-sur-Mer the woman who then, during the war, had been like a mother to me.

At the end of September, 1999, after I had long since drawn back from the ever growing *D-Day* hubbub about me, and things had quieted down around me, I received an unexpected call from an employee of the H.E.K. Creativ Verlag, which wanted to publish a new book on the subject of *D-Day*. Since they had learned that I had been there at the time, an appointment was made for October 5th. When, then, on Saturday afternoon, Frau Karin Clarissa Röhrs, an assistant, and the writer of military history, Helmut Konrad Baron von Keusgen, visited me from Schloss Ricklingen, some eighty kilometers distant, we took to each other immediately. After the customary first questions about my wartime experiences, and my comments about them, which Herr von Keusgen took down on a small recorder, we said goodbye after almost five hours *(certainly, no one had any idea of the deep friendship and relationship that would come from this meeting).* I had, to be sure, given Herr von Keusgen a great deal of truthful information, but again kept silent about the scope of my earlier actions.

We probably would not have seen each other again after this October 5th, had it not been *(just because I had reported so unselfconsciously)* that a small error had crept in that also struck him right away... Just two days later he phoned me, explained to me that he was listening to our interview on his tape recorder and that he was struck by a certain statement I had made. He asked:

"Tell me, Herr Severloh, is it your statement that at that time, on June 6th, you didn't leave your machine gun position until 1530 hours, is that right...?

I suspected I had underestimated the knowledge Herr von Keusgen had of *D-Day (only later did I discover that he had done extensive research on this subject since 1973, and over the course of those 26 years had met and interviewed a large number of veterans of the war from all the countries that had been involved. As a diver, he had even explored the sunken wreckage off "Omaha Beach" many times).* It didn't occur to me just then to do more than acknowledge his question. He certainly noticed my hesitation, and that I really didn't want to say anything more about it. However, he persuaded me to meet again on the next Saturday.

We did meet again then, almost as old friends, but I sensed that my hour of truth was immediately before me...Herr von Keusgen didn't beat around the bush, but came right to the point. He told me of a former American soldier he had previously met, in April, 1973, at Arromanches, in Normandy. This American had then gone with him to the beach in front of the site of the former WN 62, and had described to him his experiences there in great detail:

The G.I., in a small assault craft, had been brought in directly in front of our sector, *Easy Red,* toward noon. But even before the boat had reached the beach that had become quite narrow with the rising tide, it was hit in the bow with a shell *(our howitzers firing at this sector)* and torn apart. The G.I. had immediately thrown his weapon over the side of the sinking boat, and got rid of his heavy equipment as quickly as possible and had swum to the beach. There, in the fire of the shells and a machine gun, between the various articles of equipment pushed in by the tide, the pieces of tree trunks ripped from the beach by the heavy bombardment, and the mound of corpses and body parts, he labored to reach the low bank of the upper beach, only one-and-a-half meters high. When he finally got up to the beach in front of WN 62, hundreds of G.I.'s were cowering behind the bank, seeking cover from the continuous clattering bursts of the last machine gun firing down on them from halfway up the sloping coastal hillside. The Americans, many of whom were wounded, and many of whom had already crouched behind the low rise in their wet, blood-stained uniforms for hours, had not up until then been able to use their weapons to take a single shot from their exposed position. On the one hand, because the weapons were completely fouled by seawater, sand and bloody slime, and because, at the same time, they didn't dare poke their heads up over the low bank to fire. They had been able to see the muzzle flashes of the machine gun up there quite clearly, and the tracer bullets had been buzzing close over their helmets constantly. They had been kneeling between their dead comrades and cursing the "damned beast" up there...

At the end of his account, Herr von Keusgen said softly, but emphatically:

"...and the damned beast up there on the hill - that was you, Herr Severloh..."

I felt tears come to my eyes. I had really believed - hoped - that this story had been buried a long time ago. It had happened, by then, more than half a century earlier.

Then Herr von Keusgen said:

"Now that I know who you are, Herr Severloh, we are seriously interested in publishing your full story...

I resisted immediately, but he didn't back off. I looked for a reason:

"No, no, I don't want to go down in history as a mass murderer..."

Then Karin Röhrs took a psychological tack:

"Wouldn't it be better for you if you got the whole terrible story off your chest...?

I tried again to dodge:

"I'm a farmer; I can't write a book..."

She countered:

"But Herr von Keusgen is a writer... He could write your story for you..."

We met again on the next Saturday, and I began, finally, after 56 years, to tell my *entire* story. The dialogue with Herr von Keusgen took me back in my memory to the awful Russian winter, then to the delightful Legrand estate, recalled to mind my pranks, let me wander through the romantic sunken roads of Normandy, led me to strongpoint WN 62 - and behind my machine gun. Out of the grey fog of the past, the landing craft bore down on me again, let fall their ramps, and I revisited in my thoughts that awful moment when the G.I.'s hit by my bullets winced, and sank in the cold waves, or lay unmoving on the red-gold sand. There were many tears during the eight weeks of the accounting of my awful memories. I crouched once more in the trench between the observation post and the communications bunker, and Lt. Frerking shook my hand:

"Hein, you jump out next ...take care..."

On May 1, 2000, I shook hands at that very place with the man who had led me through my war experiences once again - in 22 meetings and far more than a hundred hours. He had questioned my statements deeply, over and over again; he had an understanding of my tears, and had, finally, relieved me of the great burden I had carried. We embraced. I said:

"Helmut, my "kumpel" *(buddy)*, call me Hein..."

On this day, our story was not over by any means - it only began then in earnest...

Our collaboration had already given me a great deal of pleasure in these early days, even though our subject was so serious. In March, 2000, came a complete surprise:

As usual, their Mercedes rolled up in front of my house about 2:30 PM, and as usual, I went out to greet my guests. This time, however, aside from Herr von Keusgen, his wife, Élodie and Karin Clarissa Röhrs, another, unfamiliar man of about 60 stepped out of the car. He shook my hand in a friendly way:

"Good day, Herr Severloh..."

He appeared strange well known to me. I was confused:

"Do we know each other...?"

"My name is Frerking..."

At that moment it was as if I had been hit over the head. I recognized the resemblance immediately. Then he said:

"I am Reinhard Frerking - the son..."

I was deeply moved.

Only three weeks later, Reinhard Frerking visited me with his wife and his mother, Marie-Luise, whom I had not seen for 41 years. By that time she was already 87 years old *(she died peaceful on August 28, 2002, at the age of 89)*.

Together again... From left: Christa Frerking and her husband, Reinhard, Marie-Luise Frerking, Lisa and I, in April 2000.

After the publication of the first edition of *WN 62*, I was approached almost immediately for numerous interviews and requests for information. H.E.K.Creativ Verlag managed and organized these further appearances and talks - even at so-called weapons exchanges, and with the military. My message isn't new, but it is urgent, since in times of prosperity, something like this is easily forgotten, and in that there is a great danger:

"Keep in mind that war does great harm, and only brings sorrow to mankind...!"

When I told my story publicly for the first time at a booth of the H.E.K.Creativ Verlag in an exhibition hall, I was picked up by two professional bodyguards and taken to Dortmund by car. By the time I had finished my account of *D-Day*, about fifty people had gathered in front of the booth, and listened to me in attentive silence. In a corridor of the large exhibition hall where we found ourselves, everything was at a standstill. I was asked many questions - mostly about how I handled my past psychologically. I am particularly pleased that so many young people think seriously about what I said, because what they got to hear was no superficial adventure story... In view of the extremely positive response, the H.E.K.Creativ Verlag was able to forgot the need to have me protected by bodyguards.

During the first year after the publication of my book, even more about me was reported than previously - in seven radio broadcasts and a huge number of press articles. But now, I could deal with it much better, and finally speak freely about *everything*. Probably the best article in German *(finally, for once, with appropriate depth)* was written by Herr Hans-Joachim Löwer for *National Geographic Deutschland* in June, 2002, in connection with extensive *D-Day* coverage, under the title, *Der Schütze von Omaha (The Machine Gunner of Omaha)*.

I am as astonished as I am heartened by the many positive reactions that appear continually in many publications, and often I am deeply moved by many of the letters I receive...

An extraordinary, and downright bizarre situation occurred in October, 2001, when "my" team from the H.E.K.Creativ Verlag took me on another journey to Normandy. The publishing house organized so-called *D-Day Meetings (Five day guided tours along the former invasion coast)* once a year, under the direction of Herr von Keusgen. I was to stand in the shallow depression where once my machine gun position had been

Wherever I go in Normandy, I am immediately surrounded by journalists. How they know so quickly who I am, I don't know...

139

located, to sign copies of my book for members of the study tour group. That was a completely remarkable experience for me. I was signing a book dedicated to Bernhard Frerking, the very man to whom I am indebted for having been able to survive June 6, 1944 - who had died a short ten meters from the spot.

At the entrance to the U.S. military cemetery at Colleville a French radio reporter stopped me and the publisher's team. It is often really annoying not to be able to move freely, and the superficiality and the lack of consideration, with always the same terrible questions being asked, are what continue to wound my soul.

Meanwhile, many television and film organizations took an interest in my story, and on December 11, 2002, H.E.K.Creativ Verlag sold the exclusive film rights to SPIEGEL TV. Shortly thereafter, on December 16th, I traveled to Normandy again with the Verlag team for the first filming. To be sure, I had become accustomed for some time to stand before a camera, but this work had its own completely special character. The four man crew I met in Normandy was very friendly, and went about their work with obvious professionalism. The work starting the next day was as hard as our first relaxed and convivial evening with all of them in the Keusgen's warm and rustic kitchen in Colleville.

Though a bright winter sun shone in the brilliant, blue heaven, an extremely ugly, cutting, cold northeast wind blew in from the sea over the Normandy coast usually favored by the climate of the Gulf Stream.

On the previous evening I had told the director, Herr Alexander

Czogalla, that I would only be afraid of one single scene, but he thought it would have to be reenacted: I was to stand in front of the observation post bunker, at that place in the *(still visible today)* trench where Frerking and I saw each other for the last time, then pick up some sand and tell of our leave-taking...*(Later, however, this scene was not used in the film.)*

With the film crew at the site of the former strongpoint, and at the place where my machine gun had once been located. From up here I had fired half-left into the American "Easy Red" sector.

The next day, I had, even if completely unforeseen, my chance for a "Revanche": the crew had gone with me to the sunken road behind the hill where the former Legrand estate had been located, four-and-a-half kilometers from the beach. This was where the howitzers of our 1st Battery had been positioned. The camera was set up, the sound technician stood by, ready with his large microphone, and Herr Czogalla began the interview:

"Action! So, Herr Severloh, this is where the cannon of your battery had been located..."

"No", I then replied quietly.

Alexander Czogalla was confused:

"How is that? You did say that beach was taken under fire from here..."

"Yes", I answered, truthfully.

"But then the cannon certainly also must have fired at the beach from here..."

"No", I said.

The director looked at me, surprised and annoyed:

"How is that not so, then...?

I answered him matter-of-factly:

"If cannon had fired from here toward the beach, the shells would have hit the hill..."

Alexander Czogalla tried to get it straight:

"But you have said that the cannon had stood here..."

"No", I answered again, "I never suggested that - we had absolutely no cannon..."

Czogalla looked at me unbelievingly:

"Please...?"

I explained to him, calmly: "With cannon, we would never have been able to shoot over the sweeping, hilly terrain to the beach in front of the strongpoint, but only into the first hill, since cannon are constructed for flat, horizontal fire. Out battery consisted, however, of four howitzers, and with those one could employ high-angle fire over the long distance to the beach from here..."

That same evening, I was "privileged" to sit in front of the camera for more than three hours, for yet another strenuous interview.

During the next days, the filming took place on the beach in front of the former WN 62, at the American military cemetery in Colleville, and at the German military cemetery at La Cambe - at Frerking's grave. For the whole time of our stay in Normandy I was looked after very well by "my" publisher's team - people who, in this matter, understand me the best, as they know not only my story, but also those of many other veterans, and a great deal of the entire history of *D-Day*. But no matter how much they empathize, there are moments in which no one can really understand what I am remembering and how I feel...

It came as a quite unusual surprise when Herr von Keusgen explained to me in the spring of 2003 that I had to make another trip to Normandy for further filming, and that it was for a very special purpose. This time I was picked up by the SPIEGEL TV crew and flown to Paris, and from there by train to Normandy. But first, there was a small incident at the Hanover-Langenhagen airport:

We were already cleared for the flight, were already at the gate and

At the U.S. military cemetery in Colleville with Herr von Keusgen (left) and the Spiegel TV Director, Alexander Czogalla (right). The first scene of the war movie, "Saving Private Ryan" begins here.

prepared to go the last ten meters to the airplane, when the metal detector alarm sounded as Herr Czogalla and I passed through it. Two airport officers first searched Herr Czogalla. He carried a small packet in his jacket pocket in which, aside from several old papers of mine, he had two old machine gun cartridge cases and one actually complete cartridge, but old and thoroughly oxidized. I had given him these things several days earlier, as he wanted to use them in filming my commentary. The friend of Jack Borman, the tank soldier, had scratched them out of the ground at WN 62 in 1984, at the site where my machine gun had once been placed. He had given to me then, saying:

"Here, these were yours anyway..."

Now, at the Hanover-Langenhagen airport, these old items caused a not insignificant problem. Two officers of the border patrol were brought in. Herr Czogalla tried to clarify the matter, and pointed out that the

143

cartridges were completely unusable in any case, the single bullet was very old and totally oxidized, that they had been buried in the ground for forty years - besides which, they were needed for a film. Nevertheless, the border patrol officers set it down as a violation of the weapons control law. They raised all sorts of difficulties about it with the director - and our airplane was to take off in just a few minutes...

When they wanted to search me *(the metal detector had registered on me as well)* I was able to make it clear quickly that I had *(due to an accident several years earlier)* three long metal screws in my left upper arm that held my bone together. I had, prudently, brought along an X-ray film of it with me...

After we had been held up for about fifteen minutes, we were provided a special small bus, and were able to reach our plane for Paris at the last minute. The border patrol officers had taken both cartridge cases and the old bullet from Herr Czogalla, and confiscated them. Smiling, once on the airplane, I took another of the old cartridges from my pants pocket - the screws in my arm had been sufficient grounds for the border patrol officers not to search me further...

When we had arrived in the afternoon in Paris, we traveled on by train - in which further filming was already done. In Normandy, I was then to meet *(in front of the camera)* a certain person in the early morning of June 6th *(exactly 59 years after D-Day)*. For this purpose, the Verlag team had to take me to the beach in front of the site of the former neighboring strongpoint, WN 61 - about 250 meters from a meeting place on the beach from the former WN 62. At the same time, the film crew brought the person I was to meet to the beach in front of WN 62, opposite me and even further back. Then they let us approach each other - each accompanied by a cameraman. When I then finally recognized that it was really he, whom I had not seen for 39 years, my heart went up into my throat. I felt the emotions rising within me and saw that he was experiencing the same thing. I was so excited at that moment that any clear thought was impossible. Then we fell into each others arms... - at exactly that place on the beach where he had found himself when I had fired at him with my machine gun and immediately wounded him in three places - David Silva...

What a great joy, to unite us two old men once more! The filming lasted for three days, and they were very important to us. Naturally, we had a great deal to say to each other - and they were very special words that no one can appreciate...

144

After 59 years, two old men meet at the place at which history once had placed them as enemies.

Our fate departed from the predestination of history - we became friends...

Our final visit together at the American military cemetery in Colleville was especially impressive for both of us. There I was, with a man at whom once I had fired, even though he was completely unknown to me

- only because the politics of the time had made him my enemy, in the same way that I was his enemy. We stood there between the high, white crosses of the soldiers killed in action, who had not been treated by fate back then as well as David Silva. We stood there at this well-groomed but dreadful cemetery, between the almost nine-and-a-half thousand crosses, didn't know what else to say, and each had to deal with his feelings... We walked silently through the endless rows of graves - only five hundred meters from the site of the former WN 62 and *Easy Red* sector of *Omaha Beach. (We had forgotten completely that the cameras had been trained on us the entire time.)*

After the four days of our confrontation with the serious things that had so significantly influenced our lives - David's and mine - came the most difficult moment since we had met in Karlsruhe in 1961 - our leave-taking. David had told me days earlier that he wouldn't undertake the long trip to Europe again, and so it was clear that we would not see each other again in this life, but neither of us spoke of it...

I celebrated my 80th birthday in a large gathering in Metzingen on June 23, 2003. I remember exactly the wretched state of my health in October, 1999, when I met Helmut Konrad von Keusgen for the first time. It was a great joy to me on this festive day that I had maintained my health so well during the time of our more than three-and-a-half years of intensive collaboration since then, and consider every day of that time a valuable gift. To be charged with such a great task in old age would certainly be important for anyone, and so I can also say to "my" publisher's team with firm conviction:

"If I had not met you, I would, long since, have no longer been alive..."

Photo Right Page: We were lost in thought at the 37 acre large graveyard of the American military cemetery, between the endless rows of 9,286 crosses - musings and deep melancholy. And again and again I questioned the meaning of our lives and the senselessness of our actions...

Once again at one of life's high points - and my 80th birthday; with Karin Clarissa Röhrs and Helmut Konrad von Keusgen.

Afterword

Shortly after the first edition of this book appeared in the bookstores in Germany, the response was, for me, surprisingly large and extremely positive. How it happened that the whole world discovered my account all at once, I don't know; I don't understand anything about advertising and publicity. It seemed to me that one reader told another, and one reporter told the next. In only a few months, there were a large number of press reports, as well as many radio broadcasts and, at the same time, an elaborate television documentary for the world market, under the title, *"Todfeinde vom Omaha Beach - die Geschichte einer ungewöhnlichen Freundschaft" (Mortal Enemies from Omaha Beach - the Story of an Unusual Friendship).* As a result, people from all over the German Federal Republic contacted my publisher and me. People called me up to tell me how moved they had been by my story, people who had still further questions for me, and who conveyed their good wishes. Positive reactions to my account also came from foreign countries; from France, England, Holland, Austria and Switzerland, Finland, and distant Peru. The American chief press officer of the German NATO headquarters in

148

Heidelberg even called the H.E.K.Creativ Verlag and spoke apprecia- tively about the publication. I would like here to express my thanks to all these people. It was also a great honor to be invited to a meeting with the American president, George W. Bush, and his wife at the U.S. military cemetery at Colleville on May 27, 2002. Unfortunately, however, I had to forego this short trip because of my health.

I also had some really surprising reactions from people close to me as, for instance:

I had given copies of the book to a group of my close friends shortly after it had appeared, and some time later we saw each other again. When I spoke to one of my friends about the book, a former Foreign Legion- naire, a really tough type, he said:

"A crappy book is what it is..."

I was appalled:

"Why?"

"When I read it, even I was in tears..."

But among the overwhelmingly positive reactions there were also negative reactions - two!

Shortly after the appearance of the first edition of my book the Cellesche Zeitung *(a daily newspaper of the district seat, Celle, not far from the town where I live)* carried a full page article under the title, *Omaha Beach - The Longest Day,* about *my* longest day. A few days later, a clearly older reader phoned me and snorted into the telephone that he was going to make the American authorities in Germany aware of the fact that there was a mass murderer of Americans running around free here in the neighborhood...Because of my good contacts with the Americans over many years, I have the internet address of one of their most im- portant official installations, which I then shared with the caller in a friendly way...

In the second instance, the H.E.K.Creativ Verlag received a strongly worded letter from a gentleman under whose name in the letterhead there appeared *Military History Research (without any reference to an insti- tute, and appearing hardly official - the letterhead clearly created by a photocopier).* After a lot of sweeping assertions, it implied that I had delusions of grandeur because, according to my account, *(to quote)* "the impression would be created that a large part of the losses *(of the Americans)* would be attributed to the machine gun fire of Hein Severoh *(sic)* "...The writer asserted, further, that, "those contemporary witnesses lack sufficient detailed knowledge of the situation to be able to render a suitable expert judgment"...Apparently we were all merely victims of a collective hallucination at that time, as a result of the traumatic situation; and certainly, a specialist in military history research, some decades after the invasion, knows much better than the participants what *must* have happened there on the beach. Below this letter *(with several misspellings)* the writer scrawled his name with a thick, black felt-tipped pen across the entire width of the page, in letters almost three inches high *(!)*.

Shortly after the appearance of the first printing of my WN 62, I received from Baron von Keusgen a *D-Day* Anniversary edition of the American military magazine, *Stars & Stripes,* with a reference to page 9. There I found a long statement by the former Major Werner Pluskat, who by then was 84 years old, in which he expressed emphatic opposition to slander in self-justification. He wrote that there were rumors, according to which he had not been up forward at his observation post *(at WN 59 and in the bay of Ste. Honorine, 1,600 meters east of WN 62)*, but on a private tour to Paris, and that he had lied to the author, Cornelius Ryan. *(In the U.S. war film, "The Longest Day", it was presented as if he had been the first German soldier to have sighted the invasion fleet - and from a large artillery observation bunker which - even today - is 20 kilometers further east at Longues-sur-Mer, on the cliffs of Le Chaos.)* I know that on June 6, 1944, he was by no means with his unit *(which I knew)* - that is to say, at his post. It is noteworthy, in this connection, that the anniversary edition of *Stars & Stripes* referred to here was from 1994 - six years *before* the first publication of my book...

Many of the people who write to me or my publisher seem to have one question above all others, and really to require an answer - namely, the question as to the possibility of firing 12,000 rounds from *one* MG42. Certainly no machine gun could sustain a continuous fire of that many rounds. But one has to consider the circumstances: the landing craft didn't come in steady succession, one after the other, but rather at discrete intervals, in so-called waves, and between the various waves there was often a good deal of time. During these intervals I went to the observation post bunker or the communications bunker, talked with other soldiers and with Lt. Frerking, and often we passed the time between the assaults smoking *(with trembling hands)*. I had two barrels for my machine gun and, over the course of *nine hours,* always only fired many short bursts at each landing craft that lowered its ramp in my field of fire. The barrel had enough time to cool over and over again during those intervals especially in the cold and windy weather of that terrible day. I had also, after the first longer continuous fire of over 1,000 rounds, changed the overheated barrel for a new one. A machine gunner fires only at soldiers bunched up in groups, and the G.I.'s were crowded together only at the moment when they had to leave the landing craft. As soon as I opened fire, they scattered in the water as quickly as they could. Certainly, many had tried to dodge the machine gun bursts by diving under the water, but the bullets are still very dangerous at a depth of several meters under the surface...

Regarding the durability of the machine gun barrels, I received some extremely interesting information from the internationally well known weapons expert, Volker Gremler, in May, 2004: In the spring of 1944, the Austrian weapons factory, Steyer, had produced 300 special barrels for the MG42. Because these barrels were made of the new, special Boehler Antinit steel, they were capable of sustaining the fire of 20,000 rounds. Some of them were sent to Normandy for testing...

I could, in the end, determine easily how many total rounds had been fired from my machine gun by counting the empty ammunition boxes that the unknown sergeant had brought me over the course of time from the four munitions bunkers located further down the slope of the strong-point. It also cannot be forgotten that I would never have been able to fire so many rounds had he not, all the while, continued to appear next to me with more ammunition - which also proves to me that, from midday on, I was the only machine gunner at WN 62 who was still firing. After about 1500 hours, however, I was only able to get off sporadic, short bursts, as the U.S. destroyer, *Frankford*, was firing ever more accurately at me - and the muzzle flash of my tracer ammunition was conspicuous...

Many circumstances, facts and details of the things that went on around me at that time, I learned only later. The time of my collaboration with the *D-Day*-expert von Keusgen was certainly the period during which, in general, I came to know most of the information about June 6, 1944, and about many incidents. We had traveled to Normandy five times during the years from 2000 to 2004 and had walked together on the old roads on which I had walked as a young soldier. I learned from him for the first time, that on *D-Day*, I had probably fired at the then already famous popular novelist, Ernest Hemingway, who had been brought in to the sector, *Fox Green,* in a landing craft as a war correspondent. *(13 pages of Hemingway's detailed report are reproduced in von Keusgen's* book, "D-Day 1944", by H.E.K.Creativ Verlag). Hemingway, by his own account, had approached the coast in front of Colleville in the seventh wave of the attack, toward 1100 hours. He described the problems the Americans had in combating the German defensive fire, and that many landing craft were unable, to get up directly to the beach, but instead began to circle around not far off or, as in the case of Hemingway's boat, veered off to adjacent sectors. Some, on the other hand, took wounded aboard. I had learned later, that the American coxswains *(in my field of fire, "Easy Red")* had received the explicit order to put the soldiers squarely on the beach as quickly as possible, no matter what happened; the order read:

"You are assault craft, not rescue boats!"

Why it was so dangerous for these boats to circle, I only learned from von Keusgen: the small landing craft *(scows)* were not, as I had always thought, made of steel, but rather of wood, with sides only about one-half inch thick. Only the ramps at the bow and *some* stern plates of their flat rudder housings were fitted with three-eighths inch steel.

A great deal of what happened to the landed Americans on June 6, 1944, didn't go well. There was the bad weather, with thick clouds and poor visibility, because of which the preparatory bombardment was misdirected *(too far behind us)*, and most significantly, the strong current that had forced a large number of the landing craft too far to the east - directly into my field of fire. Hemingway described very tellingly the confusion that reigned on the landing craft...I emphasize this deliberate-ly, as I would *not* wish to create the impression that I was the sole cause of the terrible American disaster of immense proportion that occurred...

For my entire life, that G.I. who had succeeded in reaching the beach down there appeared in my dreams at night. Then my rifle fire flung the helmet from his head. He remained standing for a moment, and sank on his knees. His chin fell on his chest - he died in slow motion - falling for-ward on his face on the sand of the beach...

I was scarcely 21 years old at the time. But from 0630 hours of that morning of June 6th, until 1530 in the afternoon, I had become another man - and it didn't play out differently for those poor fellows down there on the beach. But the most awful day of my life cannot simply be undone.

I am now 81 years old, and in 60 years I have not been able to rid my-self of it, the terrible and long shadow of *D-Day*, and I know that it will burden me as long as I live...

June 6, 1944, noon: Aerial photo of WN 62. The tide had risen - the sea colored by blood... At this time the flood slowly goes back. Only two landing graft drifted in front of the strongpoint. Masses of bodies of the dead American soldiers formed a dark, almost 300 meter-long border on the beach - in my field of fire (see the white lines)...

There, three French families settled down for a picnic, was where my machine gun had stood at the time; and there, exactly where I stand, Frerking and I took leave of each other for the last time...Today, children laugh here - that is the freedom and the future for which the many soldiers died at this place...

Acknowledgements

For their friendly support for the present work, my thanks to Frau Élodie H. Keusgen, Schloss Ricklingen - Frau Karin C. Röhrs, Schloss Ricklingen - Herr Volker Gremler, Buchholz - Herr Alexander Czogalla, Hamburg - Herr Reinhard Frerking, Langenhagen - Mister David E. Silva, Seven Hills, USA - SPIEGEL-TV, Hamburg - Mister Joseph P. Rivers, Normandy American Cemetery ABMC, Colleville-sur-Mer - National Archives and Records Administration, Coll. Park, MD, USA.

I extend a special thanks to the author, Helmut Konrad Baron von Keusgen, who, as my "Ghostwriter", found the right words for my account!

Heinrich Severloh

Photo credits

Photographie's

Helmut K. von Keusgen:
Pages 9(right)-13-55-71-80-140-141-145(2)-147-155(2)
Élodie H. von Keusgen:
Pages 14-126-139-143(2)- 148-157
Volker Gremler:
Page 154
Lisa Severloh:
Page 111
Heinrich Severloh:
Pages 40-43-75-97(2)-104-110

Archives and private collection's

National Archives and Records Administration, Coll. Park, MD, USA
(Signal Corps and Air Force):
Pages 57-61-62-64-65-67-68-69-73-84-86-87-153
Normandy American Cemetery ABMC, Colleville-sur-Mer:
Page 118
Helmut K. von Keusgen:
Pages 53-59
Lina Wernecke:
Page 74
Heinrich Severloh:
Pages   9(left)-12-23-24-25-27-28-29-32-34-38(2)-44-45-46-49-92-94-
97-106-115-117-120-122-128-131-134-138

Obituary
by Helmut Konrad von Keusgen

At his last meeting with the press: Hein Severloh on May 3, 2004 at the age of 81, and already marked by physical frailty - and still more reflective...

Heinrich Severloh died on January 14, 2006 at 7:25 AM in a retirement home near Celle.

His health had been declining drastically since the beginning of 2004. During the spring there were, but only occasionally, periods of apparent improvement. On May 3rd of this year, four weeks before the 60th anniversary of the invasion, Hein met with the press for one last time - in a quite small group. In a conversation with me afterward, he admitted to me that he could no longer take part in the large celebrations in Normandy - and that he no longer wanted to. In concluding, he said:

"In my old age, I have been able to experience something wonderful through you, and it has been an honor for me such as I never could have imagined. That with my terrible war experiences I can still leave behind an important message for those who come after me, gives me a great deal of satisfaction. But now, there is nothing more for me to do. Let others go to the *D-Day* spectacle - I don't need it any more, I have accomplished everything..."

Now Hein is gone... and the completion of this new edition was not without emotion for me. We had become good friends in the more than six years, and in view of the serious subject matter, the sun did not always really shine on our relationship. We visited each other very often, were in Normandy many times, and I walked those paths with him that he had once trod as a young soldier - as well as those at WN 62 - on June 6, 1944... The similarities of our character made it possible for me to understand him well, and was the best qualification to work with him and to develop this book. I am very lucky to have met this extraordinary man - and now I miss him...

Perhaps Hein Severloh will meet those men again where he now is, whose lives he defended then, as his own - and to whom he owed another 62 years of life. I hope that Hein now lives in a better world, in which there are no soldiers and no machine guns...

January 19, 2006: In a sea of flowers, a last rew
that had influenced all of Heinrich Severloh's lat

David E. Silva passed away Novew